M000196100

SYNDICATING IS A B*TCH

SYNDICATING IS A B*TCH

And Other *TRUTHS* You Haven't Been Told

Bruce "Apt-Guy℠" Petersen

LIONCREST
PUBLISHING

SYNDICATING IS A B*TCH

And Other Truths You Haven't Been Told

ISBN   978-1-5445-0606-7 *Hardcover*

978-1-5445-0604-3 *Paperback*

978-1-5445-0605-0 *Ebook*

978-1-5445-0673-9 *Audiobook*

Disclaimer: I am not a CPA or an attorney. To do any of the things in this book, you need to consult your own legal and financial experts. This is just my personal experience having done this sort of work for years.

CONTENTS

INTRODUCTION

Right off the bat, I have to tell you: this isn't going to be all rainbows and lollipops.

I tried to be as honest as possible in the title of this book, but since you picked it up anyway, I'd guess you're one of two people. Either you've been burned before, or you've got stars in your eyes. Somewhere, someone told you how syndication is the way you can make your millions, and you're sold.

I'm not trying to scare you out of syndicating. The problem is that I've talked to hundreds, maybe thousands of people who are interested in the syndication model, and only 20 or 30 percent are truly equipped for it. If I can shed some light on the difficulty and stress that comes along with it before you decide to jump in, then I will consider this book a success.

You might think that there's some magic key that I and I alone can offer to unlock your pathway to easy money. But there are no sparkling unicorns to guide you through your first deal. There's no checklist that will *guarantee* a smooth or even successful syndication for you.

I know that's not what I'm supposed to say. I'm supposed to be this guru person who gives you a secret formula and makes promises with a vague "this isn't necessarily indicative of what will happen for you" attached just to stay on the right side of the law. I'm supposed to tell you about the yachts and the ponies and the $20 million homes.

Except you've heard all that bullshit before.

How many times have you gone through this with someone, usually in real estate, making all these promises...just to find out the successes are really just their best-case scenario? How much money have you spent only to find out that they glossed over reality and are just making money off of you and thousands of others who have taken their course? That's not to say all of those people are bad or dishonest; in fact, most are good—but many of them don't have your best interest in mind. That's not their objective.

That's not what this book is about anyway.

This book is about what it's really like to bring investors

together in a syndicated purchase, and the kind of person you have to be to make that work. Yeah, there's incredible earning potential on the other side, but without knowing what you're actually getting into, you're almost guaranteed to lose. Big.

SHIT WILL HIT THE FAN

You don't really have a way of knowing whether I'm going to be real with you or not, so I'll start with a story. One about how $5.2 million completely disappeared, right at the end of a syndication deal when everything was supposed to be set.

Let's go back to August of 2016. Everything about the apartment complex that we were buying in San Antonio had checked out. Our investors were lined up. We had completed our due diligence inspections and made it to closing day. Austin, where my wife and I live, is about an hour and a half from San Antonio, so we wired our $5.2 million for the purchase at about nine in the morning on a Friday, then made the drive down there to hang out in town until we received notice that the wire had been received. It typically only takes a couple of hours for a wire to go through, so the timing was going to be perfect.

By eleven, we were at the property and ready to meet with our newly inherited staff. The night before, the previous management company had taken all of the computers and phones out of the office, so there wasn't much for anyone to do. The staff could physically walk visitors through the model unit and show them the amenities, but that was it. Since the wire was delayed, we couldn't do much either. Still, we figured it would be there any second and decided to go ahead and set up all our new computers and phones and begin training them on our management software.

Around 11:30, I started getting phone calls. "Bruce, where's the wire?"

I sent it at nine, should be there any minute.

Thirty minutes later: "Bruce—still no wire."

Now, I'm an eternal optimist, so I wasn't exactly worried, but this wasn't normal. I needed to do some digging. So I called the bank, assuming that's where the disconnect was. But the bank didn't have the money either.

The wire had definitely gone out shortly after nine that morning. As far as I could tell, all of my investors' money was gone.

I collected supporting documents, tracking numbers, and confirmations, hoping that would keep us moving—I didn't have anything more than that to offer the sellers. The money was in my account, and then it was gone, and somewhere between there and the seller, it was nowhere to be found.

At 4:30, my attorney called me for the last time that day: "You have to get out."

Without the successful wire transfer, the property and staff weren't mine. I didn't own it yet. The process is normally so sure at that point that I hadn't told anyone the sale wasn't finalized—not even my wife. She'd been running around training the staff on our management software all day. No one else needed to worry about this thing that should've been resolved by now. But it was clear by that point that nothing was closing that day, and we had to go.

I now had to tell my wife that we didn't own the property. We had to explain to the staff that the closing didn't clear— and that we had to take our computers and phones with us. We couldn't leave everything there over the weekend without knowing what was going on. They had to call the old management company back to figure out what to do. Before we left, someone showed up, dropped a single box with one phone and one computer on a desk, then turned around and walked out.

With the staff able to do at least part of their jobs, my

wife and I packed up and drove straight to a restaurant for some food and some liquor. Needless to say, having $5.2 million disappear is a little bit stressful. I maintained most of my optimism—surely someone could figure this out—and by 5:30 it paid off. Sort of.

Here's the thing: when money is wired, it runs from one bank, through the Federal Reserve, and to the other bank. Usually, it's a simple and quick process. In between, there's a division of the US Treasury Department called the Office of Foreign Assets Control (OFAC) who has the authority to make a pause. They're charged with watching for money laundering and have a list of known bad actors throughout the world that they run against the participants of wires to see if anything pops.

Turns out, the name of the property we were *trying* to purchase was also the name of a known bad actor in Columbia. Since my proactive ass had already filed the DBA (doing business as) paperwork to match our investment group to the name of the property, guess what name was on the $5.2 million wire? Yep.

OFAC had flagged it immediately *and had been under no obligation to tell us.*

After one more terribly uncomfortable explanation—an email letting the investors know their money was gone and the property wasn't yet ours—our Friday night had ended.

All eventually worked out, though. By Monday morning, we finally got word that the wire had been released, and we were finally good to close. Done—with a little bit of unneeded stress!

If you think you can handle that kind of excitement in your life, keep reading.

WHY I WROTE THIS BOOK

Writing isn't really my thing. I've had to teach myself to enjoy reading, and even then, it's more like a task I know I need to do than something I think I'll enjoy. But this topic really had to happen in a book. It's a chance for me to be candid with you and get into some details that I might not be able to at a networking event or speaking engagement.

More importantly, it's a chance for you to explore syndication from the safety and anonymity of your own home. When you show up to a conference or something, it's way too easy to feel pressured into things. That either gets people into trouble or keeps them from showing up at all.

There's no risk here. There's nothing keeping you from getting a little bit more information. You might find out syndicating isn't for you, and for many of you reading, I want that to be the case. I'd rather talk you out of something that's not a good fit than to get you in over your head. Unfortunately, I've seen that happen to people—in fact, it happened to one of my closest friends.

Without exception, every single time for probably a year or better, he'd blow me off for lunch or happy hour or whatever we had set up. Something was obviously wrong, but I didn't know what. He wasn't talking to me about it, though, so I let it go. When we finally caught up, I found out that he had tried to get into real estate after witnessing my apparent success with syndication. Unfortunately, he got involved with one of those gurus that you've probably encountered as well—you know, the ones that promise the world.

That system was bound to not work. And of course, it didn't. But he didn't know any better, and he wound up losing money. Now, I want to make it clear that not all of these programs are crap—some are really good, in fact. I just want you to understand what's going on when you are sitting in the room with these folks and listening to their "pitch." There's more to understand about syndication than just finding a property and raising the money from your friends.

I can't help but wonder who else is out there, feeling taken advantage of by someone heavy on promises and light on details. The promise of easy wealth sounds great, and the high-pressure pitch is hard to turn down.

I can't help but wonder if a book like this would have helped him—or you—out. I had to write it.

DO THE WORK

To make syndication as clear and simple as possible: it's the pooling of capital by multiple investors to invest in something. It doesn't have to be real estate—hell, you could syndicate a candy bar if you wanted to. I'd like to syndicate a baseball team. But one of the most common and accessible fields is real estate syndication, which I've been doing for years now.

I've had investors decide after a deal or two that they can do what I'm doing and syndicate their own deal. I've also had people who were interested in leading a deal find out they were better off as silent investors.

What I haven't seen much is interest from friends and family members, especially in the beginning.

One friend that I've known for over twenty years asked me early on, "What are you going to do if it doesn't work?"

I had just gotten started, and he already decided it wasn't going to work by his words to me. That I needed a backup plan. I was pissed. Looking back, I don't fault him for this. It's the way most people are wired—they need a contingency plan, because they're pretty sure it's not going to work and to be fair, he had seen other endeavors of mine not work out. It's the one-foot-out concept, or not being fully committed. If this is going to work, as Tony Robbins says, "You have to burn your boats." He just wanted to make sure I'd be alright, and he meant well.

It just hit me the wrong way when it happened because I had truly not considered the possibility that it wouldn't work. Not even once. Real estate investing and syndication works. I learned from others who had made it work. Why the fuck would it not work for me?

Syndication is all about scale. It's taking a purchase you would have otherwise made on your own—like a single-family home, a duplex, or outside of real estate, maybe a small business—and blowing it up to much bigger proportions: an apartment complex, an organization, a sports team.

It's a lot of leg work and networking to coordinate, and for your first deal, you're going to be pulling a lot of strings and wearing a lot of hats. But the first deal that I did brought a 300 percent return on our money. That kind of turnaround will turbocharge the shit out of things. (Disclaimer: I bought that first deal in 2012, so much of that profit was economy driven. But had I not taken the plunge, I would never have gained that 300 percent.)

The more deals you do, the more you can scale. Now that I've done this for many years, I can hire people to do a lot of the leg work. My existing properties truly only take about two hours a week of work, no exaggeration. My wife and I give ourselves a raise every time we do a new deal and pay almost no taxes because of the nature of investment real estate. We choose when we want to do a deal and when we want to take a break. Our life is our own.

In short, we listened to a mentor who actually knew what they were doing, and we *made* it work. There's no if. There's no maybe. There's only the question of whether this is a good fit for you—whether you're willing to do the work.

Listen, I'm the kind of person who can figure shit out. If I work hard enough and long enough on something, I know it'll work. I'll outwork just about anybody and do the things most people don't want to do. In the past, when I worked in retail and tried to start other businesses, that got me in trouble. Most jobs will take advantage of a person like that. In syndication, that inner drive makes it work.

You're also going to need some hefty risk tolerance. Syndication is business ownership. You're the final gatekeeper. You go down with the ship. There's no passing the buck here. You're the dude. You can work harder than anyone else in creation, but if you can't handle putting your name on the line, you're not going to make it.

All that work and risk is a means to an end. It gets us to balance and sanity much quicker than working our asses off for someone else. Financial independence is hard to come by these days, and for the right person, this is a way to get there.

By the way, that guy who wanted to know my backup plan? He came around. He actually wound up investing with us and was shocked when he actually began to receive his quarterly distributions. Go figure!

THE WHOLE TRUTH

You might have already noticed that my word choices don't always match your average investment professional's. I'll go into more detail later about what it means to be a professional syndicator, but it doesn't mean being someone you're not. This is how I talk.

Please don't get hung up on the words. I'm a genuinely caring person who just wants to help you—and the words are just words. Read this book for the information that it provides and the person underneath: my goal here is for you to know the truth. Syndication is incredibly lucrative. It's the most rewarding thing I've ever done in my life. And it's not for everybody.

In fact, it's not right for many, if not most people. I want to make sure you know exactly what syndication truly is so you can go into it with your eyes wide open. If you still want to do it once you know what you have to put in and where it could kick you in the gut, please go for it. You might even want to come to one of our in-person seminars for a weekend to ask intensive and specific questions and get more prepared for your deal.

Those weekends have nothing to do with my business model, though. I've got no skin in the game here. You won't do me any favors by doing a syndication deal, walking away—or even by buying this book. Anyone who tells you they're going to make money off a book is usually wrong. That's not why I'm doing this.

I just want to help you see behind the curtain. I want you to know what's really going on without having to wade through the hype and the sales pitch. I want you to find a path out of the normal, everyday grind without being roped into someone else's often empty or overly optimistic promises.

I want to see you become fabulously wealthy, and maybe syndication will be your way in. Or maybe it won't be. There's only one way to find out...Keep reading!

CHAPTER ONE

A WAY OUT (AND UP)

When I was around thirteen years old, I saw an ad in the business section of the paper—why I was reading the damn business section as a teenager, I have no idea—for a bank that offered around 8 percent interest rate on savings accounts, compounded monthly. I didn't quite understand what it meant, but I was fascinated with money, and I wanted to learn how to grow it. So I called them up to learn more. It was probably a teller who answered, but I didn't care. I said, "I'm looking at this ad. Can you explain what interest is and how this compounding thing works?"

That's a good indication of who I was as a kid. I was the one with the lemonade stands, selling baseball cards, selling comic books...I don't know if I was consciously trying to "get rich" or not; it was more that I had an entrepreneurial streak. Maybe something clicked in me when I got home one day and a Toys for Tots box was on the porch—when I thought for the first time, *Holy shit, we're poor!*—but I don't think that was it. I don't have the story that talks about how I knew I was poor and was determined to make a better life. My mom was such a fantastic single parent that being poor was never at the forefront of my mind. In fact, I didn't even realize we were until that Toys for Tots box showed up.

Honestly, I think it was something completely different than that. I was simply fascinated with the *game* of money. I liked watching it grow and making things happen.

I kept playing the game when my father passed away, just after my high school graduation, and left my sister and me roughly $20,000 each in life insurance proceeds. I took it to Merrill Lynch and opened a brokerage account. I was seventeen (and I needed my mom's help since I was a minor).

At first, I wasn't thinking about how that interest in money could turn into a career. I was just playing. When it came to my future, I thought of two things: being the mid-'80s, everyone said you have to go to college, and everyone said computers were the thing to learn. So I went to college for computer programming.

I didn't have a computer. I didn't know much about computers. I didn't make great grades or particularly want to go to school, but those were the things I was "supposed" to do next. Hell, I barely made it out of high school and somehow I thought college was a good idea?!

Needless to say, I hated computer programming. It just wasn't going to work out for me. Even before I made it out of my core classes, I decided to switch to a finance degree—not that it mattered. I was still a bad fit in the formal and structured world of higher education who hated school.

Thinking ahead to the day I would be free of classes, an ad for a stockbroker job caught my eye. I figured it would be a good chance to practice the interview process so that when I got my degree (how naïve I was to believe I would actually stick around that long!), I would be ready to get a job.

And then I got the damn job!

TRYING TO PLAY BY THE RULES

Surprise! As a stockbroker with no degree, I was just a salesperson. It wasn't any more of an "in" for a financial career than walking onto a car lot and interviewing as a car salesman. There were no prerequisites required of me other than they liked my personality, and I could pass a couple of tests to obtain my series 7 and 63 licenses.

Unfortunately, my personality was not well suited to the kind of sales they wanted.

I thought I was becoming a stockbroker to play the money game. I thought I could get that Porsche that all the other douchebag brokers around me were driving. But I couldn't make myself be a douchebag broker—and apparently, that's what they were looking for. I hated the culture they had created around high-pressure calls, yelling at people, calling them names, challenging their egos, and pushing them into purchases. There was no way I could match that intensity. Not like that.

When Desert Storm hit roughly a year in, my decision was made for me. Everyone stopped buying stuff, and since I was paid solely on commission, that meant I stopped making anything. I had to quit—with no skills, no degree, and no income. I picked up some work as a bank teller for a few months, barely scraping by at $200 a week, but that didn't cut it either.

That's when retail got me.

I understood retail. I liked retail. It's black and white, with clear parameters. Get in there, bust your ass, work visibly harder than anybody else, and you'll be rewarded. The work I did was directly connected to my money in hand.

I *didn't* love the hierarchy and structure.

There were times when I felt like I wanted to buck the system. For a little while, I worked for Home Depot, then eventually got fired because I was the rebel employee in that particular system. Instead of going right back into retail, I spent a little while stretching my entrepreneurial wings—could I play the money game without being tied down to their restrictions?

I knew the store employees back at Home Depot were always looking for good assembly companies to build their grills, wheelbarrows, sheds, etc., and it was something I enjoyed. So after I got fired, I got all my paperwork in place and set up as a vendor and began assembling items that they offered to the customers "fully assembled." It was a decent little business, but not quite enough.

Next, I picked up a job at Bed Bath & Beyond, but that draw to do my own thing kept nagging at me. While still working there, I played around with other businesses on the side. For almost a year, I ran a commercial cleaning business that cleaned offices overnight. Hated it. Then a buddy told me about how real estate agents send out thousands of pieces of mail every month, and how he knew someone who made $3,000-$5,000 a month just to run that mail through sorting, stamping, and sealing machines for them. So I rented a space, bought mail service equipment, and gave that a go. That didn't get me anywhere either.

Retail was the only thing that made sense. I knew I was good at it, and I could do the work, make the money, invest it, and watch it grow. Do more work, get more money.

For years, that's what I did. I was the single guy willing to do anything to get ahead. I literally ran everywhere I went. I worked harder than everybody around me, and it paid off. Every time I got promoted, I got a 10 or 15 percent raise. Sure, it came with more responsibility, more hours, more stress, but it felt more like the money game than selling stocks had. The harder I worked, the further up the chain I went. Work turned into money, predictably and reliably.

In spite of the hours, I loved the work. It felt good to be the best and be rewarded for it. It felt good to lead a team and see tangible results. But even when you love something, your body can only take so much.

After a few years of promotions, proving myself, and pushing harder and harder, I was now a store manager and working 80- to 100-hour weeks. I didn't know how much of a toll that had taken on me until I took a short vacation to Rocky Mountain National Park. When I came back, I wasn't rested or invigorated. I was exhausted. I felt physically sick going back to work. The last straw was an upset customer backing me into a corner when my patience was too thin to handle it well. I knew this was likely the end. I absolutely am a people person—but I had worked myself down so hard that I now found them to be nothing but an annoyance. I was done.

It was time to go. I went to my boss and told him I had to be done or I was going to jeopardize my store and my employees. It's a good thing I did because he had already pulled my file and was ready to come to me. So I gave my two-week notice and left.

This time, I didn't jump into anything new. I was 100 percent done with working for other people. And I didn't have to anymore.

For twenty years, none of that overtime had gone into extravagant vacations or a big mortgage or a fancy car loan. Everything I needed had been paid for in cash, and all of the extra had gone into my side hobby—the money game. My account had about a half-million in it, which was just enough to withdraw returns and live for a little while until I figured something out.

That's when the money game got serious.

QUESTIONING THE RULES

I don't know your exact story, but I can guess. You've probably got a 401(k) or an IRA or savings of some sort. Maybe $500,000 like I had, but probably at least $100,000. You have that much because you've worked your ass off too. You worked that much because that's the bullshit bill of goods we were all sold.

Go to school. Work to the bone for forty years or so. Wait for it all to pay off when you're sixty-five or seventy. You are likely not in top health to enjoy the fruits of your labor, but congrats! You win the American Dream.

There had to be a better way.

Most of the time, this grand life plan doesn't work. Maybe you realized it in 2009 when half your net worth disappeared. Maybe you're holding your breath, afraid you'll be downsized or laid off before the payoff hits, and then what? The job market will go for the twenty-year-old willing to make $60k with all the newest education, which might be half of what you're used to making now. So you hold your breath, work twice as hard as anyone else, and hope you make it to retirement without any hang-ups.

Or maybe you're looking at sixty-five more realistically the closer it gets—who the hell wants to wait until then for the payoff? If you're working as hard as I was, you'll be too worn down to enjoy it.

I walked away from retail with no other plan because nothing—*nothing*—is worth hating your existence.

Why follow the traditional path when you might not hit that magic number, and even if you do, you'll have to use it on a Rascal scooter? I'd much rather make sure that what I do will get me to that retirement number now, at forty or fifty years old, when I can enjoy it.

A lot of us in this position look into real estate. Traditional wisdom has something to say about that too. Usually, we think about taking our own money and buying one or two rental houses or maybe a six-unit apartment complex that can take the edge off our basic income needs.

Syndication takes that traditional approach and blows it up. It's how you can buy fifty or a hundred units, as many times as you want to. You're a hard enough worker. The question—the first of many—is whether you're willing to step outside the box to make this work.

QUITTING THE GAME

If all you have set aside is a 401(k) or traditional retirement plan, you're putting money away that you hope might grow at 6 or 8 percent for forty years, which will (also hopefully) then be enough to live on for the rest of your life. If you want the "rest of your life" to start before you're sixty, you'll likely have to deal with a 10 percent penalty plus a shitload of taxes.

Assuming you're well enough to enjoy at least the first half of retirement, welcome to the new game: watching your account dwindle. It's a race to the death, where you hope you die before you run out of money. Honestly, what the fuck kind of life is that?

Think about it. The traditional retirement route all but stops growing as soon as you quit working. It's not easy to find a fund that will replace as quickly as you need to withdraw. If you have to live off of a 4 percent withdrawal rate, you have to have a steady 5 percent growth rate or more. If the market corrects even at 20 percent, your fund is going to take a huge hit that it might not recover from. Assuming all goes well with your fund, is that $5 million you hope to have at retirement going to last if you live to ninety? Ninety-five? Or if healthcare costs keep skyrocketing?

I had to re-educate myself on all of this too. We're told as soon as we start working that the 401(k) is the way to go. Why? Because it's what the boss knows about. It's what the financial advisors talk about. It's what the government favors. Honestly? It's not what the billionaires do. Not even close.

Why the hell are we not doing what the billionaires are doing? If you want to break from tradition, you have to shake off middle-class habits, investment patterns, and expectations. Some of us struggle with the idea of making a lot of money and leaving the middle class behind. It might be connected to fear or to shame or to simply not knowing what to do. All of that has to go. Wealth is how we get shit done. It's how we create jobs for other people and create purpose in our lives and affect other people for good.

HOW TO WIN

Real estate is appealing for its returns and the streams of income you can create with it. It's tangible. We have control over it. But I don't have to sing the praises of real estate to you. Plenty of other people before me have done that. You are probably here because you're already convinced that real estate is your way out. What I want to give you is a way out and up—*way* up. Syndication is real estate on steroids. Not just real estate, either. The possibilities are literally endless.

One of my goals is to turn my lifetime love of baseball into syndicating a minor league team. I love everything about the game, including the numbers and stats behind it. Honestly, that's part of what I love about being a syndicator and sponsoring deals. I'm a numbers guy. It takes a lot of number-crunching to make sure we can keep the doors open, keep everyone employed, and keep everyone housed and fed. With every new deal, I lean on the stats and averages and percentages with the same enthusiasm I had as a kid reading the backs of baseball cards. To take that passion full-circle into eventually owning my own team...that's something special.

Sure, I want to give the kid in me that gift. I can even think of a handful of ways that owning a jet would be great for my family, my business, and yeah, that inner kid too. But my goals are bigger than that. I also want to create a better life for my daughter.

My daughter is twenty-three and living on her own, and she is autistic. Throughout her childhood, it was difficult for her to fit in around the other children and in the typical childhood experience. In ninth grade, she got tired of being bullied her whole life and dropped out to finish high school at home. My wife, Stephanie, helped her finish and get her GED, but it didn't get better. As an adult, she still gets picked on, laughed at, and bullied. She doesn't have much of a peer group or a community to rely on.

One of the goals my wife and I are working toward is to

create an autistic or special needs apartment complex. Care for special needs children and adults is insanely expensive, so rent would operate on a sliding scale. It would operate as a nonprofit, and almost like a dorm or a senior community. We have all kinds of visions of help with chores, shuttles, and a space to feel safe and connected to each other.

Because we have the money syndication provides us, we don't have to worry about the means to make it happen. The wheels are in motion, and we can focus on the logistics.

How much in your life have you missed out on because you didn't have the means? What could you dream about and accomplish if you could make a couple million dollars every single year? That's why we syndicate. That's why we go through the shit to make all of this work.

In the next chapter, we'll look at exactly what syndicating is, including the fact that you can work syndication into any kind of purchase at all. It's definitely not exclusive to real estate, though that's what I have experience in and will focus on in this book.

For now, know this: I can teach you what syndication is and what it might do for you. I can show you how to break off of this bullshit traditional path you feel stuck on. I'll give you the basic blueprint that helped me walk away from hundred-hour workweeks forever, secure my retirement, and earn more than I thought possible. But I'm not here to fix all of your shit for you.

Your success is not my responsibility. It's yours and yours alone.

This isn't an easy path. It will take time to get your feet underneath you. It will take a certain kind of personality. It will take a financial investment, which might mean parting with some of that precious 401(k) and all of the dogma you've swallowed about what that means.

But it's way fucking easier than giving forty-five years of your life to someone else and still not knowing whether you'll survive.

CHAPTER TWO

WHAT IS SYNDICATION?

The official, *Merriam-Webster* definition of a syndicate is: "a group of persons or concerns who combine to carry out a particular transaction or project." That's a good start. You might have heard of the term *crime syndicate* or of *syndicated television*. I assume you have some form of an interest in syndication and that's why you picked up this book, but don't worry if this is the first time you've heard of it. Lots of people haven't, including people in real estate or other industries where syndication deals might be useful.

Let me put it in my own words: syndication is a group of people coming together to put money into an investment, which will be managed by one person or one small group for the benefit of the larger group.

From an investor perspective, that means you and some other people are giving money to the operating partner (Deal Sponsor) who will orchestrate the purchase and run the operation. All of your profits come from that operator's actions. If you're a syndicator, you're the operator and orchestrator of the *business*.

You can syndicate a baseball team, an apartment complex, or a Snicker's bar if you really wanted to—though the returns might not be great.

Syndication changes the way we think about what we can invest in. The next time you leave your house, look around at the apartment buildings in your area, from single units to the massive projects. They were probably purchased in one of three ways: institutional investors like hedge funds, billionaire families, and insurance companies; wealthy individuals, who can sometimes manage to afford smaller buildings; and syndications.

On your own, you might not look twice at a multimillion-dollar apartment complex. But through syndication, you might only have to invest $20,000–$50,000 to get in on it. More on that in a minute. The point is, once your eyes are opened to the potential, you'll start to see these buildings everywhere. Not just the massive, brand-new complexes that are probably owned by the institutional investors, but buildings you've never looked at twice. In my neighborhood, within a half-mile radius of my house, there are probably twenty apartment complexes that average between twelve and twenty-four units. Those are all someone's investment, hiding right there in plain sight.

It's not just what we can invest in that changes with syndication, either. The returns are different too. A great stock market return might average out to be 6–8 percent over an extended period. My syndications, on the other hand, usually return 15–25 percent per year (when averaged out over the entire hold period, including the profit on sale), paid out regularly in an extremely tax-advantaged way.

Let's take a few minutes in this chapter to get familiar with syndication as a concept and what it means for you and your investors.

HOW TO MONETIZE SYNDICATION

As the syndicator—the deal sponsor—you go out and find a deal, then find investors to get the money together for it. You set up all the lending and move through the "due diligence" period where you double-check all of the numbers, inspect it, and make sure it looks like a profitable investment, and then you make sure it gets to closing. If you decide sponsoring the deal isn't for you, there's always investing. Many if not most syndicators put their own money into their deals alongside the silent or passive investors, so you will probably need a decent amount of seed money to get started.

Throughout this book, I'll walk you through syndication on a real estate property, specifically an apartment complex. You'll see it from the syndicator's side and get an idea of the investor's side. I fully expect most of you to decide to invest in someone else's deal first.

I personally jumped right into being a deal sponsor first. I had the time—sitting around living the Dave Ramsey life on my stock returns, never spending a dime and wondering what might come next. I had the money—with a half-million in my account and twenty-plus years until standard retirement, I could use the $115,000 that my first deal required (it was important to me to be the largest investor in my first deal) without feeling the pinch. And I had someone to mentor me. Those are all important components to have in place for your first deal.

Most of us don't have the stomach to do something we haven't done before, and few of us have a sizable amount of money available to start as a sponsor. So most folks are going to start as a passive investor, treating this like a stock market investment with a bigger upside. That's fine. Investing passively first means you get to see how it works. If you still want to be a syndicator by the end of the book, starting as a silent investor is a great idea to get a feel for the flow of a deal.

If you're ready to become the syndicator, there are a few ways that the sponsor can be compensated. All of it is optional. You don't have to charge certain fees or structure your deal in any specific way. Still, this should give you an idea of the different ways we're compensated for our work.

ACQUISITION AND DISPOSITION FEES

A lot of work goes into getting a deal under contract and closed. The syndicator has to come up with earnest money, juggle paperwork, oversee and pay for inspections, and more—and sometimes it happens multiple times before you can actually get to close. To compensate for that work, you can build an acquisition fee into the deal.

The acquisition fee is typically 1-4 percent of the purchase price, which you can imagine might be a very high number. If you are purchasing a $20 million asset with a 4 percent acquisition fee, that's an $800,000 fee on the day of closing.

Granted, that rate is on the high end, and you won't be doing deals that big for a while, but it's not an unrealistic scenario. I've got a friend who is raising a $50 million fund for multiple assets with a 4 percent acquisition fee. Once he deploys all of the capital, he will have made $2,000,000. That's how lucrative this can become.

The disposition fee shows up on the other end of a deal when it's time to sell. There's not as much work involved in the sale of a property as in the beginning purchase, but it's still a lift. Now you have to send the property around to multiple brokers on behalf of the partnership. You gather their assessments and get an idea of the sale price. You get your financials in order and have everything ready to give to the eventual buyer. The compensation for that effort is the disposition fee.

Usually, the disposition fee is in the 1–2 percent range. A common arrangement is to have a 2 percent acquisition fee and a 1 percent disposition fee. This disposition fee comes out of the sale price, as a cost of closing, directly to the syndicator, typically before the profits are split between the investors and syndicator. Another somewhat common fee is a refinance fee, which will range between 1–2 percent.

Keep in mind that for the syndicator, these fees are not real estate dividend income. They're earned income, directly connected to compensation for a service. That means they are taxable right then, at the next quarterly filing.

PROPERTY MANAGEMENT FEE

This is the fee for managing the property itself. Most of you will hire an outside company to handle this for you, and you will pay this fee to them. If you do decide to manage the asset yourself, you will pay your company this fee—which will range between 4-10 percent of all collected income paid monthly on smaller properties, up to about one hundred units. Once you pass one hundred units, 3 percent seems to be the norm. Your lender will likely insist that you hire an outside experienced property management company on your first deal or two.

If you decide to manage the property yourself through your own property management company, you will be the one hiring the onsite staff and overseeing them.

Asset management, with or without managing the property yourself, isn't a passive position, either. You are sending regular updates to your investors, sending out quarterly distribution checks, and heading any meetings you might need. You're also working with the lender to stay in compliance with your loan documents. The asset management fee compensates you for all of that headache.

ASSET MANAGEMENT FEE

As the asset manager, you will be managing the management company as well as working with, communicating with, and raising the capital from your investors. You will also be working with the lender to get the deal closed, as well as managing ongoing financial reporting and compliance while you own the deal.

Basically, you are managing the acquiring entity, or LLC, that will directly own the real estate itself.

This fee is usually between 1–2 percent of all collected revenue paid monthly.

As you have probably noticed by my using the words *typically* and *usually,* these fees can vary as they are negotiated. These are just guideline amounts.

Since we're talking about your first deal in this book, I'm not going to get into the specifics of how to self-manage.[1] Few banks will give you that option right now—though you might have the leeway in your loan documentation to switch to self-management after some pre-determined length of time. Be clear about what your limitations in the loan are and stick to them, or the bank *could* call the loan and want all the money back. That's a mess you don't want to find yourself in.

---

1   With that said, I do manage my own properties through a separate company that I've started. It's definitely an option, and I might slip into some self-management language throughout the book since that's my experience.

THE PROMOTE (OR OVERRIDE)

There are so many variations to the compensation structure that we could probably write a book on those alone. But I'm not a lawyer and don't have any interest in getting that detailed. So the last one we'll get into is the "promote." It's yet another way you can be compensated for the headache, liability, and stress.

The promote is taken from the profitability of cashflows, from sale, if you do a cash-out refinance, or any other time cash goes out to the partnership. Basically, if cash goes out, the promote is paid.

If a promote structure is set up as 80/20 (a common split), 80 percent of all distributed cash would go to the investors, and 20 percent would go to the syndicator. It's your way to make a living, otherwise you wouldn't be able to do this.

Typical promote structures are 80/20 or 70/30, though I've seen them as high as 55/45 and as low as 90/10. In any case, the larger number will typically go to the investors. If you invest as well, and you probably should on your first deal or two to add to your investors' comfort level with you having no experience or track record, you would also have your share in the 80 percent. The promote doesn't interfere with it at all. If you invest 10 percent just like everyone else, you'll get the 20 percent promote, plus your pro rata share of the investor distribution. You are effectively selling 80 percent of the company to the investors, so the 10 percent you contribute is buying 10 percent of that 80 percent—or 8 percent in total. In this example, you would receive 28 percent of all distributed cash each time it is paid.

PREFERRED RETURN

The preferred return is compensation for the investors only, not the syndicator, but I want to cover it quickly because it affects deal structuring and is a consideration you'll want to make. To understand a preferred return, let's say we have $100,000 in profit to distribute to the investors. In our example above, the syndicator takes their $20,000 promote right off the top of that amount before the rest is distributed to the investors. A preferred return protects some investor return, even if that means the promote can't fully be covered.

If the preferred return is set at 6 percent, the deal sponsor won't get their promote until the preferred return (6 percent per investor) has been distributed. Now, it's not strictly percentage-based. Once the investors hit their minimum required return for the year—or if the preferred return on that distribution has been satisfied—then the promote becomes the priority again before any added returns are distributed. A preferred return is not a guarantee in any way; it simply states that the syndicator/ sponsor won't get their promote until the limited partner investor gets their 6 percent.

The preferred return is especially helpful on your first deal because it acts like another comfort level for your investors as they are taking a chance on you. It can hurt returns for the syndicator, but it can reassure the investor that the system is working in their favor. The syndicator doesn't get rewarded unless the investor has gotten a minimum return first.

Again, these compensation structures are not the be-all, end-all, exhaustive summary of revenue streams. You and your attorney can work out all sorts of things to get you and your investors paid. But now that you have a basic idea of the framework, you can go into those conversations with a little more understanding and confidence.

TAXES: THE AVOIDABLE EXPENSE

If you're going to get into syndication, think about it like a business. Because that's what it is, even for real estate syndication. You're not buying a property or becoming the owner. You are managing the LLC, backed by silent investors, that owns the property. When you look at the benefits and drawbacks of syndicating, your reference point should be against other ways to be an entrepreneur more than it is about other ways to buy things.

If you have looked into business ownership like I did, I'm willing to bet "tax advantage" caught your eye a couple of pages back. This is a huge benefit of investing in real estate, and I promise it isn't a shady trick or some hidden gimmick. It's just the nature of our tax system.

Very simplistically, IRS rules around depreciation give you a certain amount to deduct every year. It happens for houses and smaller properties too, it's just on a bigger scale for bigger properties. That "loss" counteracts the amount you made on the property, and only the profit is taxable.

Not all businesses have depreciating assets, so this isn't something everyone knows about. It isn't something everyone can take advantage of. You can't depreciate inventory—this is something retail just can't touch.

Even after the year-to-year benefits, there's more. Syndicated real estate investments are usually set out for a limited amount of time—say, five to ten years. At the end of that time or if the market indicates it's time to move, it's understood that we will sell the property and split the profits up however the documents says to. When that happens and I get a sudden pop of income from the sale, I can roll all of those profits into another investment to defer that tax hit, too. This is done by utilizing a part of the tax code referred to as a 1031 exchange. There are very specific rules around these exchanges, so please consult with your tax strategist or CPA to see if and how you can qualify for the 1031 Exchange.

It's no coincidence that real estate is treated so well by our tax code. Rich people make our laws, and a large portion of rich people got rich off of real estate or invested in it once they got there.

Depreciation and 1031 Exchanges are just the start— and you can't do this with a W-2 income. For example, you can't write off the clothing you wore to present to a room of people (unless it's specific clothing required by the employer). Even if you make a $1 million as an employee, you're still just an employee. When you have a business, on the other hand, the write-offs start rolling in. Every time I travel to network, check out a property, or meet with investors, it's all a business expense that I write off on my taxes.

What's cool about it is even if I were taxed like everything else, I would still stick with real estate syndication based on the returns alone. You just can't beat them. The tax breaks are just the icing on the cake.

TIME AND MONEY: UNAVOIDABLE INVESTMENTS

Tax breaks are nice, but this kind of scale doesn't come

without a cost. If I had to narrow it down, to really be able to syndicate, you have to make time, front money, and have the right personality to make it work. What does that really look like? It varies from deal to deal and absolutely gets easier the more deals you have under your belt.

Your first time out is absolutely going to be the hardest. In the beginning, you're really just trying to educate yourself. Every little step is a learning experience, and sometimes that feels like fumbling your way through.

If you're still working and aren't ready to give up your job, you might not be ready to devote the time needed to your first deal. My first property took about twenty hours a week in the beginning and probably for the first six months after the deal closed. I was there quite a lot, overseeing the rehab, building an office that the property needed, sitting with the staff and property manager I hired, and going over the business with her. At a bare minimum, I had to be on the ball every time the phone rang. That's still true.

You have to be able to get documents and answers to the lender while working on your loan and the close process. You have to be available for walkthroughs, meetings, and inspections. You're on a tight timeline to get everything done. If you're tied down to someone else's schedule at another job and can't answer a personal phone call, I don't know how you could make it happen.

I believe this should be your primary, maybe even *only* responsibility, at least at first. I realize that's not possible for everyone, but you'll need to devote as much of your time and attention as possible to that first deal. I know others that have made having a full-time job and doing their first deal work, but it's extremely tough and I don't recommend it. This is another time when an investor might not feel comfortable investing with you if this isn't your full-time gig. Whether that means taking a sabbatical to get your first deal or investing in others until you have some income to live off of until this takes off—don't think you can do this while you're still in the office fifty to seventy or more hours every week.

This brings us to our next unavoidable investment: money.

Your first deal is almost never going to pay for all of your living expenses, especially when you have a family, and that doesn't include the cash you have to have up front to make it work at all. If you don't have much cash to draw from, you won't make it through earnest money, inspection fees, and up-front (though reimbursed) costs needed to get to closing. You'll be completely screwed if the deal falls through and you don't get reimbursed, too.

Unless you're one of those freakishly charismatic people who can get people to fork over millions of dollars without any kind of display of mutual trust (like investing in your own deal)—this is not a zero-down, get-rich-quick thing. A solid 99 percent of the population doesn't fit that bill. So you're going to have to put some money in.

For example, you might start with a twenty- to forty-unit property, which is on the smaller side, and you decide that investors need to come in at a minimum of $50,000. You should probably come in at that minimum or higher.

Investing in your own deal shows how much you've bought into it. It makes you part of the process that they're going through too, and it also builds on your return.

Investment money aside—we'll say $50,000—now you have to think about the up-front money to get the deal closed. There will be earnest money, roughly 1 percent of the purchase price. For our million-dollar example, that's another $10,000.

Then there are inspections for the structure, plumbing, roof, wood-destroying insects, all of that—all out of pocket. And don't forget the attorney fees all along the way.

This basic scenario is how my first deal took six figures out of my pocket before I ever saw a dime. All of the up-front fees will be reimbursed by the business after a successful closing. But don't count on it, just in case something falls through. You need to be comfortable putting your own money up to sponsor the deal. Shouldering that risk is what earns you the income that a syndicator gets.

THE *YOU* FACTOR

Everything you do in life will have some risk involved. Even working for someone else holds some risk, and I would even argue more risk as you're at someone else's mercy for your paycheck, even when it feels like the stable choice. Whatever you invest in—the stock market, gold, oil, property—carries risk and comes with no guarantees.

I can't say it enough: if you can't handle this kind of risk, you shouldn't be doing this.

Know who you are and what you're comfortable with. Don't lie to yourself about this. The purpose of this book is to make you aware of the mechanics of syndicating and what it requires of you. Only you can decide whether it's a good fit.

Risk tolerance isn't the only match you have to make, either. You have to be able to find and orchestrate *people*. Not just investments, but the people behind them. If you ask yourself, "Who am I?" and the answer comes back, "I'm a dick," you shouldn't do this.

You might laugh now, but get really self-aware and then come back and tell me if it's still a joke. Someone actually told me once, "I really want to do this, but the thing is, I'm a dick."

Well, okay then. This isn't for you—and good luck getting anybody to let you invest in their deal either. Nobody wants to work with a jerk on either side of the deal.

Your investors should like and trust you enough to be able to work with you. You should be able to network without turning people off. And then their trust has to pay off by you handling the ups and downs of owning a business without losing your shit.

SQUARING WITH THE RETURNS

The risk, liability, stress, and work that goes into syndication can be heavy. If something has turned you off at any point in this chapter—whether it's the time or money or personality it takes to do this—you probably want to keep reading from an investor's point of view. Sponsoring a deal might not be right for you.

If those basic prereqs haven't scared you off, you might be wondering why on earth anyone would go put up with all this shit?

Here's a test of your mindset. How do you react when I say this: Any time I want a raise, I just buy more real estate. Contrast that to telling your boss you "want" a raise and see what happens. I just go buy another property. Period.

If you're still in that middle-class frame of mind, you might be cringing a little (or a lot). Money is supposed to be evil, right? Except we have all sat in someone else's office year after year on our review dates, hoping for a 3–5 percent raise, and maybe managing to pull off a 3 percent cost of living increase.

Business ownership means being in control of your own income. Your own destiny.

Syndication means taking that control and scaling it. The day I started syndicating, my net worth was around $500,000. Within three years, it jumped to $5 million. Why? Because I'm willing to take on the risk, liability, and stress of sponsoring these deals.

We do it for the scale. We do it because we want to claw our way to freedom. We want to work for ourselves and to serve our investors, staff, and residents. We do it because we want to generate wealth that will leave a legacy. We do it because it's not another damn vendor gig or mail processing service or cleaning company.

We hand over that time and money early on, knowing that we can soon free up time and money to do what we really want to do. I do it because now I have daughters, and one of those daughters has autism, and my wife and I dream of creating something lasting for her and her peers to enjoy an independent, safe, and supported life.

In other words, we syndicate for the same reason anyone else starts a business: freedom. It just feels more accessible to start those businesses. We can see the investment and know what it would look like to win or to fail. That's why there are so many tech startups every year, even when we all know how many of them fail. Anybody can go out and give those businesses a shot. The risks and benefits and paths to success are clear.

I want to make syndication that clear for you. I want you to know what it takes and what it can earn you. If you don't succeed, that's alright. You knew what you were getting into. If you do it right and do it well, though—damn! You'll scale it faster than most any other business can. The bigger you go, the easier it all becomes.

And hey, listen, if you only have the intestinal fortitude to be an employee, that's fine. There's nothing wrong with that. Just know this: your own business can't lay you off or refuse to give you a raise. Find another sponsor, get an investment of your own in there, and enjoy the returns and tax advantages that real estate investing can provide.

CHAPTER THREE

START WITH A PLAN

Before we get into any details, I have to issue a disclaimer here: each deal is its own game with its own curveballs to figure out. Your first deal might not look like mine. You might move faster or slower, and you might run into more roadblocks or sail right past things that were difficult for me. Your first deal won't look like your second or third deal, either. The best I can do is to give you a general idea of the important steps to take and things to remember. You have to stay flexible and be willing to learn on the fly.

Apartments are definitely not the only thing you can syndicate, either. The details I'll use throughout this book will come from my experience in apartment syndication specifically, because that's what I know. But the underlying principles can give you an idea of how to run a deal in just about any scenario.

I'll use my experience, my examples, my stories—but don't take it as a blueprint or some kind of limitation that says you have to do it like me. Every deal is different.

One thing you have to do no matter what, though, is plan.

For my very first time syndicating an apartment complex, I backed into figuring out what I wanted. I knew what I felt comfortable trying to raise for my first time out gathering investors. I knew what size property I wanted and the rough age of the property I was looking for. I knew it needed to be something I could get to within an hour or so of my house. I knew I wanted it to be in a neighborhood that was relatively stable and secure. So I set all of those parameters (which we'll talk more about later on) and just started looking.

Within a few months of watching the market and touring property after property, I landed on one that checked all the boxes.

Some syndicators might not find a deal so quickly. If you live in a town with two hundred people and have to drive six hours to get to the closest city, it'll be harder to find something that works. Don't just go after whatever is available. Set yourself up for success by making a plan and sticking to it.

In this chapter, we'll look at the main parameters that

can keep your hunt for a deal on the right track: location, condition and risk, age, and price.

WHERE SHOULD YOUR PROPERTY BE?

The first time you sponsor a deal, you're more or less proving yourself. The bank doesn't know you can do it yet. Your investors don't know you can do it yet. It's not going to be easy to secure a loan and raise money for a big property that will put a lot of true dollars in your pocket, even if the return is fantastic. The bank is your biggest partner, and you're their biggest risk. They won't let you go buy three hundred units completely unproven.

My first property was a forty-eight unit. My second one was 120. From there, I landed 256-, 192-, 292-, and 200-unit properties. I went as quickly as the lender would let me and as I felt comfortable with. I never wanted to overextend myself or move more quickly than my organization could keep up with. With each deal, I learned more and grew more as a syndicator so that it got easier rather than harder. A mentor and even a good mortgage broker can give you some direction and help you pace that scale. That's also why you have to have the breathing room—with both time and money—to get the first deal in the books. Otherwise, you might feel pressured to build recklessly just to make enough to live on.

What does time and money have to do with location? Pretty much everything.

STAY CLOSE TO HOME

Let's break first-time income potential down for a second. We can make all the numbers easy just as an example: let's imagine you decided to syndicate a ten-unit property at $100,000 per unit. The total cost was a million dollars. To get your first deal, my rule of thumb is that it's going to take approximately 30-40 percent of the total purchase price in order to cover a down payment, closing costs, operating capital, and any rehab money your lender won't let you roll into your loan. So for this example, you and your investors will be in for $300,000. Everything goes smoothly, your up-front money has been reimbursed, and now it's time to look at returns.

Let's say your ten-unit property generates about $2,000 a month (as a very broad rule of thumb, $200 in free cash flow per unit will be close), and you'll get about $400 of that free cash flow or "profit" per unit off the top—that is, your 20 percent promote from earlier in the book. The remaining $1,600 will be divided up amongst the investors. If you, as an investor, put in 10 percent, that means you'll get another $160 a month. That's it. You're probably looking at about $500-$600 a month while you get your feet under you with your first property.

Now, the math stays the same when the property changes. The same scenario for a hundred-unit property would bring you $5,000–$6,000 per month—much more reasonable in terms of income and budget. You might be able to get in the door for more the first time around if another syndicator—who has experience in the asset class you want a loan for—will cosign the loan for you. The bank will be happier with that added experience in the deal, but your cosigner will need to be paid for the risk they are assuming, even though they will likely be silent in the process itself, and you'll have a bigger property to figure out your first time through. It's not ideal.

Bottom line: first-time deals are smaller, and so is first-time cash.

It's important to keep this in mind—remember, this is not "get rich quick"—when you pick your first property's location. So you can say now that you're fine with driving three, four, five hours to get to it, but be real. Are you going to make that drive three or four times a week in the beginning? Are you going to make that drive for $1,000 a month or less? It might be fine in the beginning when it's new and you're excited, but that's not going to last.

If you burn yourself out like that, you'll wind up walking away. The deal will die, you'll throw your hands up and say it didn't work, and you'll never do one again—all because you chose the wrong first deal. Now, some of this can be overcome by hiring a third-party management company, but you still need to be able to get to the property on a fairly regular basis to ensure the management company is doing a good job.

For the relatively low amount of regular income you'll make on that first deal, stick to properties that are close enough that you can get to them for all of the back and forth necessary to close a deal. Stick to properties that are close enough to check on even after the property management company takes over the day-to-day, on-site tasks.

THRIVING AREAS ARE STABLE AREAS

When people in central Texas look into buying their first property, invariably, they'll come to me, all excited about their find.

And it always seems to be in Killeen, Texas.

Why do they find Killeen? Because it's the cheapest in the entire area. It's the cheapest for a reason, and I almost always tell them to keep looking.

Here's why: you want to skip over any areas that are overly reliant on a single employer—and that includes the military. Killeen is home to one of the nation's largest military bases. What happens if there is a mass deployment where a large portion of the military people take off and the spouses move to be closer to mom? Also consider, who are the burger joints or grocery stores going to serve if a ton of the town's population suddenly disappears? Or, to get even closer to home, think about January 2019 when the government shut down for over a month. If it had extended even a week or two longer, a lot of properties that are overly reliant on government employees would have been in trouble. Loans are due whether or not rent is collected, and everyone from the military to federal employees to welfare recipients were affected. This can also be the case in an area too dependent on any one employer or industry.

Smaller towns that have one employer creating 10–20 percent of the workforce are at risk too. What happens if the company shuts down or closes the location?

Now look five years down the road when it's time to sell your property. If the town is stagnant, what do you think property values will look like five years from now? They'll probably be right where they were when you purchased the thing, and you'll have to sell it at the same price you bought it for. That's not why we invest in real estate.

If you're trying to narrow down locations within an accessible distance, go for the thriving, growing communities whenever you can. Go where the young people are moving, not where they're leaving. As soon as a kid graduates from a dump of a town with no opportunities, they can't wait to move. Even the good towns lose kids to cities like LA, Austin, Nashville, and New York.

If you're not close to one of those towns, one indicator of a growing area is how good its tech industry is. If they have a vibrant startup or tech industry, they're likely going to draw in highly skilled, highly paid people.

Another indicator is the median household income. You want to buy in an area where median income is equal to three times your rent or more. If your rent is $1,000 a month, average annual salaries should be at least $36,000 within a mile or two of the property. That's the range where people can comfortably pay rent, and rent is what keeps your asset alive. The more above the three-times in income you can get, the easier job you will have in attaining the higher rents you may be counting on.

I can't really get into what rent looks like specifically, but I can tell you that location will play a role. A shithole town in south Texas might have really nice units renting at $.60 per square foot, while Austin is such a hot market (everyone and their brother wants to live there) that the baseline average is $1.50. Meanwhile, San Francisco could be double even that.

Cool spots with a lot to do draw more people in to live and work and rent *your* properties.

By the way, I'm lazy and don't like to do a lot of unnecessary research, which means I buy in my own backyard whenever I can. I know everything about this area and where I do and don't want to buy because I live here. Because I'm in Austin, that works for me. It might not be the case for you, so plan on doing some heavy research for any location that you're not already deeply familiar with.

WHAT SHOULD YOUR PROPERTY BE LIKE?

Every investment has some kind of risk categorization. You have to know what you're getting into before you make the leap. For real estate, there are graded classes of risk. Those grades are subjective—your A property might be my B+—but there are some rough parameters that can help you compare properties, convey generalized risk to your investors, and communicate with your team about the property.

A C property will generally have a pool and sometimes a business center and fitness facility. B properties and above will nearly always have a fitness facility. An A property will usually be ten years old or newer. These are the new to newish properties that catch everyone's eye with all of the best amenities. An A property will have everything the B properties have, plus maybe even a dog groomer, game room, or movie theater on site. A-level properties are also going to cost more—though the exact amount varies widely by region. In general, the higher up the class schedule you go, the higher the rent will be per square foot. The logic also follows that higher-end tenants and newer buildings with less rehab turn into a less inherent risk.

As you go down-market, the buildings get older and the rents start to drop. Down in the C and D level properties, things are going to break more often. Lower rental rates draw rougher crowds who can be harsh on the property. They're also more likely to default, get evicted, get fired, or get arrested. Going down-market requires a higher return in order to get investors who are willing to take that risk—in the 7-9 percent range on a C compared with a 3-5 percent return for A properties (these examples are from 2019 and will likely vary through different economic cycles).

PROPERTY GRADE	RISK LEVEL	EXPECTED RETURN
A	Low	3-4 percent
B	Medium-Low	6-8 percent
C	Medium-High	7-9 percent
D	Highest	10+ percent

Everybody wants to buy an A property. That's trophy shit that you show all your friends.

It's also not realistic for most deals, not to mention your very first one. Usually, you won't be able to raise enough money to buy one—think about how many of your investors would need to put in $50,000 or more to make that happen—and then you have to deal with that narrow margin of return. If the market corrects when you don't have a lot of headspace, your loan will be at risk.

On the other end of the spectrum are D properties. As a rule, I stay away from the D properties, which are the ones with dogs running around off-leash, cars on blocks or abandoned, and zero curb appeal or amenities. For me, no return is worth the risk in a D neighborhood, although I know people that specialize here and do very well. This is part of the "know yourself" and have investing criteria and stick to it. There's usually a higher projected return, but don't kid yourself, there's a very high likelihood that it's going to kick your ass. They're not only pieces of shit, but they can also be dangerous. You don't want to deal with someone pulling a gun on you when you go ask for rent. It doesn't have to be on the ritzy side of town, but do you feel safe there? Would you send your spouse there at night? Is it drawing in people who will reliably pay rent every month? D properties don't typically answer "yes" to those questions.

The cheap sticker price is enticing, but don't let it fool you into buying. The two or three extra points of return aren't worth the stress they cost. You'll lose your mind trying to control that asset.

Start off with a little bit of an older property in a working-class neighborhood (even if it's not a trophy that you can brag about) and make some steady money. This will likely be a B or C level property—C for most people. They're usually more affordable, the return is good, and they aren't so high on the risk meter that it becomes dangerous.

WHAT KIND OF MONEY CAN YOU RAISE?

The specifics of how to raise money will show up in chapter 5, but you have to get a starting point in mind. All you really need to know right now is how much money you feel comfortable raising—and that you're going to have to get soft commits for two or three times that. Not everyone who says they are interested will be able to show up with money when it's time to close. This isn't personal, and it may not be a problem with your skills. It's just the nature of investments and timing.

Think about your network, or how your network is growing. Let's say you have twenty people who might be good for $10,000–$30,000, plus the $50,000 you planned to put in. You figure you can manage about $500,000 in total cash. If we use that rule of thumb that you need 30-40 percent of your first deal in cash, you can buy a roughly $1.25-$1.65 million property, assuming you raise what you think you can.

That's your target. But keep in mind if you think your target property will take roughly $500k to close, please get soft commits of between $1-$1.5m.

Now, here in Austin, the cheapest property you'll find (that's not so rough that you don't want it) is probably going to be $80,000 per unit, or "per door," as it's usually referred to. At that price, you could probably get a fifteen-unit place or smaller. In San Francisco, it might only be a four-unit, which isn't multi-family, by definition.

Without backing into this investment number, you might spend a ton of time scoping out the exact right location and property—only to realize it's way outside of your budget. The trick is finding a deal that you can *afford*, that also has the right wage demographics, growth, safety, employment, and risk level.

Remember, you won't always have to be this selective. After two or three deals, you'll be able to buy damn near anything you want as long as you have the capital. You'll have the experience and the chops that will get you loans and bring your investors in. It's like compound interest in that it tends to grow exponentially. The first deal is the hardest and pays the least. The more deals you do, the easier it is to raise money, the easier it is to get lending, the bigger and better your properties can be.

Ironically, the bigger the properties get, the easier it is to manage them. Scale is not just about income but about having the people, experience, and team to take care of things as they come up. The extra "doors" or units create a margin of both money and resources that means you can all breathe easier day to day.

Of course, this all begs the question, what happens if you can't get all the checkboxes to line up to make the first deal?

Well, you have to raise more money. You have to take longer to raise that money. You have to find a place with cheaper prices. You have to do what it takes if it's really what you want to do. *Move* if you have to. You may not be living in the right market for the kind of deal you need. Maybe you can't afford to break into your local San Francisco market, or you're looking at properties four hours away to find a reasonable deal. In a case like that, it's less likely to happen. You may need to move.

Be real with yourself. Understand who you are and what you're up for. There's nothing wrong with *not* wanting to move, work harder, fundraise, or whatever it's going to take to get a deal. Just understand that it means deal sponsorship/syndication isn't for you right now. Save yourself the headache, hassle, heartache, and loss of money, and wait until you're ready to do this the right way.

If we've passed another milestone here and you still think you're game for syndicating your own deal, keep reading. Next, we're going to talk about the team you need to assemble to make this shit happen.

CHAPTER FOUR

ASSEMBLE YOUR TEAM

Welcome to the next milestone. I've tried to scare you off, but you're still here, ready for more. This next step is a difficult one for a lot of people. Everyone tries to go out of order in the beginning. They're taking stabs in the dark, trying to decide which comes first, the investors or the deal, *ready, fire, aim*!

I've got news for you. There's more groundwork to do before you're ready to pull the trigger. The first and most important step is assembling a team.

Sure, you could try to do this by yourself. I won't stop you. Of course, it's really damn stupid to do that. You're going to lose your ass and then talk about how "real estate doesn't work." That's not true. It's not real estate or syndication that's the problem. It's you trying to do something without anyone else's help or guidance.

Since I'm a baseball guy, I think about the second baseman showing up for the game alone, without the other teammates, and expecting a good outcome. You just can't do it as the lone second baseman. If you don't have everyone in place on your team, you'll never be able to come up to bat, much less hit that grand slam deal you're hoping for. (Word of wisdom: my approach is to hit lots of singles with the occasional double, and if I hit enough of the singles and doubles, I have a better shot at nailing that grand slam. I try to approach this business conservatively to make sure I have my "bases" covered and build off that stable foundation with a hopeful grand slam or two along the way.)

In this chapter, we're going to build out your roster. Who has to be on a team to make a deal work? We'll put them in a batting order—who's your lead-off guy? And as long as you're taking the right steps forward, you can work on building your potential investor list in the background because they're part of your team too. In fact, they're the most important part of this whole thing. You'll never stop working on your investor list as long as you plan on doing more deals.

Pulling together a syndication deal requires a lot of juggling, a lot of moving pieces, and a lot of communication happening all at once. It's not linear, necessarily. You can't keep your blinders on until one step is done. Your job is to be the coach, making sure everyone is prepped, on deck when it's time, and ready to go as soon as they're up to bat.

One last word before we get started: don't flake out and go cheap here. Don't go to Legal Zoom for an attorney or H&R Block for your taxes. This is way more complicated than that. You need specialized, experienced professionals on your side who practice in this exact field day in and day out. You will have to pay them. And they will make your life so much easier because of it.

IT ALL STARTS WITH THE INVESTORS

A quick note before we get started: nothing happens without investors. As soon as you decide that you're going to do your first syndication, finding investors should be your top priority. Build your database, and then keep building it as long as you plan on working more deals. The last thing you want is a great property to pop up with no one to turn to for funding.

The next chapter is all about networking, building your database the right way, and connecting with people you can turn to when it's time. In this chapter, we'll walk through the other team members you need to bring on board too—just don't forget that investors are needed at the same time.

TRY TO FIND A MENTOR

Listen, not too many years ago, I weighed 240 pounds at five-feet, nine-inches tall. I was fat as hell and tired of being that way, so I thought about what my life looked like and what I could do to change it. After those hundred-hour workweeks, I was too exhausted to make dinner or do anything at all. I'd get a burger, eat it in front of the TV, and pass out on the couch. Clearly, I had a few problems to work out.

When I stopped working for other people, I didn't have the "no time" excuse anymore, so I could stop eating all those burgers. That doesn't mean I ate *well*—there's still pizza, ice cream, and donuts after all. But I did make a change. However, when that change didn't lead to weight loss, I decided it didn't work. So I tried a different approach. I started walking, which got me in a little better place, and I got off the pizza and pies, which also helped...but it still "wasn't working." Never mind the fact that I was eating half a gallon of ice cream every twenty-four hours. I had made *a change* and didn't have results, damn it!

It wasn't until I got a trainer that things really started to change. I cleaned up my eating habits, exercised, and dropped a hundred pounds of fat.

My health suffered for a long time while I tried to fumble through trial and error. If you tried to trial-and-error your way through a single-family deal, you could lose tens of thousands in one pop. If you tried to do that in apartment complexes, you're talking about hundreds of thousands, if not millions of dollars. Real estate mistakes are expensive. Syndication mistakes can be devastating.

I'm going to teach you how to syndicate a deal, from a very high level, but this is still just a book. As soon as you start building relationships to assemble your team, they're going to know you're new and have only learned from a book. Having a mentor on your side can help make the transition easier.

By the way, being new is not a bad thing. Don't ever lie to someone and act like you know more than you do. My point is that you need a trainer. Reading this book is like reading about a healthy diet. You actually have to put these plans into action, and that's a hell of a lot easier when you have someone to support you and advise on your specific circumstances. Find a local mentor who has done this successfully before, whether it's a paid company or someone who just wants to show you the ropes. Get in touch with someone in person who can give you a hand.

We're all busy. Most people don't have the time to nurture a brand-new mentoring relationship, and no one owes you that time. Just keep your eyes open as you network and get into these investment spaces until you find someone who can and is willing to help. You might go to investment meet-ups and find someone who can't help you themselves but knows another person worth getting in touch with—something like, "*You know, I know this guy Fred who doesn't come to these anymore, but you might want to get in touch with him.*" Look for someone who you click with and, most importantly, someone who knows what they're doing and has experience syndicating their own deals successfully or, at a minimum, has bought their own without partners.

If all they have done is one deal on a six-unit property, that's still more than you. They have insight that will help you avoid pitfalls, connect with team members, and step into this with a little bit more vision. If someone like that has some time available, take it. Listen to them. Learn from them. Your deals will be smoother because of it—not totally smooth, but better.

Try to get someone in your corner to help you out like this early on, as soon as you start working on your prospective investor database.

REAL ESTATE LISTING BROKER

→ Role: Curates listings, markets properties for sellers, facilitates property tours, communication liaison between seller and buyer
→ When to find: Right away
→ When to engage: As soon as you identify the parameters for your target property
→ Type of interaction: Relational, ongoing
→ Type of expense: Commission-based at time of sale to be paid by the *seller*

Early on, your search for a real estate broker will be very low impact. Go to websites, get on email lists, and that's it. Most brokerage websites have some parameters that you can start with, like where you're looking to buy, roughly what size and age of the property, what kind of asset you're looking for—all of the stuff we worked through in the last chapter.

They want to know what kind of properties to share with you, and if you're not selective, you're going to be overrun with potential properties. Then again, if you try to dial it in too tightly, you might not get much flow at all. You might get one or two deals a week, even one or two per month, depending on where you are. Try to strike a balance and get that information flowing.

The info you get from a few broker mailing lists will give

you enough to start assessing deals, which we'll get into next chapter. When a property looks like it might fit your parameters, you'll be able to raise your hand, sign a digital confidentiality agreement, and get the financials and offering memorandum that they've created for the property. You don't have to tour a single property to get your feet wet assessing and selecting potential listings.

When you're ready for a tour, you can reach out to the broker directly. Based on the properties they send out, the way they communicate, and how you connect with them, you'll settle into a working relationship with your brokers. After the first deal, or even after you do a tour or two and they start to get a feel for exactly what you want, that relationship will change. They'll have a better idea of what you want and will start to keep you in mind as they find and list properties. Keep several people for each of these disciplines in your Rolodex, including the real estate brokers, because not everyone will have access to all of the deals that are out there. Cast a wide net to get as much deal flow as you can.

When you reach out and make that connection, be honest about where you are in your syndicating journey. Brokers might not be excited about working with someone who is new, and you can bet that they won't take a single call of yours if you are full of shit. Don't misrepresent yourself to get in the door.

Everyone has to start somewhere, so be honest about who you are and where you are in the process. They should take you seriously, without you lying and saying you've done a dozen deals already. Let them know who you're learning from and how, what kind of support you have in place, but that this is your first deal on your own.

This is not your damn Instagram account—you can't filter your experience. You can't co-opt your cosigner's or mentor's experience as your own. These are sophisticated professionals who work with buyers on these large deals every single day. If you bullshit them, they will walk away.

And of course, the golden rule: *don't be a dick*. Brokers talk to each other, and if you're a dick, you'll never get another one again.

You can't do this without a good listing broker, not without making way more work for yourself than you need. You're the tadpole in this pond. Don't ever lose sight of that. You're looking for a mutually beneficial relationship. You're here to prove yourself, and one day they might trust you enough to bring you the best deals. Until then, you're here to learn.

MORTGAGE BROKER

→ Role: Shops around loan options for you and presents you to lenders

→ When to find: Right away

→ When to engage: As soon as you know you want to do this for sure

→ Type of interaction: Relational, ongoing

→ Type of expense: Fee-based at time of sale

Your mortgage broker is your number one advocate. They only get paid if they get a loan for you—usually one percent, sometimes split between them and the end lender, but if you hit $10 million, that's a great payday for them—so they really want to make that happen. Instead of dealing directly with the end lender, you'll primarily work with the mortgage broker.

You can technically find a mortgage broker from a basic Google search, but more likely it will come from your network. Whenever you're at meetups and real estate clubs, talk to people. If someone has a few deals under their belt, find out who they use and what their experience has been like.

The mortgage broker will work to create a pre-qualification letter for you to let you know what you might qualify for, which means they need some information when you reach out to them. They need a personal financial statement showing your liabilities, income, and assets. They won't lie for you, but they'll want to present you in the best light possible.

Of course, it won't be your income alone that qualifies you for the loan, but they want to know that you're real. If you get cosigners or guarantors who are worth $10 million and you're worth negative—and a lot of people are—they're going to have a hard time getting a loan for you. They might not even be as willing to work hard for you as they otherwise would be. Show them what you can about yourself, then have a conversation about your plan to syndicate, how much you believe you can raise, and who might be willing to sign with you on the loan.

In other words, this relationship starts with a "getting to know you" conversation. They want to know what you want to accomplish, what you have to work with, what kind of guarantors you can bring to the table, and what those people look like financially.

For your first deal at least, go for a broker who works nationally and has access to many lenders across the country. These won't be junior brokers who just got a license and decided to go for it—they are experienced and have a huge database to draw from. Syndication deals can be more difficult to source. Someone with only a few banking relationships won't be able to help you the way they could with three hundred banking relationships.

The bigger they are, the more deals they've done, the more connections they have, the more likely they are to find an option for you.

Last but not least, I'll say it again: don't lie, and don't be a dick. If you lie on your personal financial statement, what happens when it's time to prove it for loan underwriting? There's no way to get away with that crap, so don't. Own up to the fact that you've never done this before, because they'll figure it out anyway. It's better to find out at this stage that you won't be able to get a loan than finding out after your earnest money and attorney costs are already out the door.

REAL ESTATE ATTORNEY

→ Role: Drafts your offers to buyers and helps in the contract negotiations
→ When to find: When you start looking for properties
→ When to engage: When you want to submit a letter of intent (LOI) on a property
→ Type of interaction: Transactional
→ Type of expense: Fee-based at closing—potentially up front for your first deal or two. $5,000– $20,000

The real estate attorney comes up to bat from the time you are ready to put in an offer and stays in the game until the day of closing. They're doing all of the back and forth on contract negotiations and redlining it, they're pulling background information and overseeing title searches and surveys, and making sure the purchase stays on solid ground. Their main role in your world is to protect you.

Like many of these teammates that you find, the real estate attorney can likely be found online, but it's best to get someone through a direct referral. Talk to people at meetups, ask around about their experiences. I would shy away from someone who has only worked on single-family transactions as they are different and usually not as complicated.

Once you have done a few deals with a real estate attorney and you have the reputation for reliably making it to close, you may not have to pay anything up front. Their fees will come out at the closing table. But unless you have someone in their network who can vouch for you, you'll probably have to pay up front, per hour for their work at the beginning. Depending on the size of the firm, that could be $250-$650 an hour, or $5,000-$20,000 at the closing table.

Don't cut corners just to save that cash. If you tried to do this stage yourself (and you're not already a real estate attorney), the industry will not take you seriously. That's like the idiot who stands up in court and says, "I will represent myself." Don't be that guy. You can't tell someone who owns a $10 million property that you want to buy it and you're going to be your own counsel along the way. They'll laugh you out of the room before they take that deal because they know it's going to be a train wreck. Hand the responsibility over to your real estate attorney and let them protect you and your deal.

The more you work with one person in this capacity, the more they'll understand you and what you expect in contracts—what is of high importance and what might not be that big a deal for you. It's like going to the same doctor over and over again. Eventually, they'll know more about you than a new guy will, and that will help you get better service faster. You can have multiple people lined up in case they're needed, but a long-term relationship is definitely beneficial for ongoing work.

SYNDICATION ATTORNEY

→ Role: Crafts your syndication deal

→ When to find: When you start looking for properties

→ When to engage: When your LOI is accepted

→ Type of interaction: Brief but thorough relationship

→ Type of expense: Fee-based, $7,000–$20,000

While the real estate attorney handles the contracts and closing process, a separate attorney has to work on the offering you present to investors. When you have a property that's moving forward, you're ready for a syndication attorney to help you craft the framework of the deal between you and your investors.

Some attorneys have a real estate division as well as a syndication division, which might be helpful to keep everything in-house. If yours doesn't, look for a syndication attorney the same way. Network, ask around, and get referrals.

Your first call will take a half-hour to an hour for their "getting to know you" process. They'll want to know how to structure the deal, which will take some discovery. This is where the compensation structures from chapter 2 come in. Usually, they are good about helping you fine-tune the details as long as you start with a general idea of what you want.

A good syndication attorney is a sounding board and counsel. It's their job to understand what you want and let you know when it's not a good idea. Mine still has these conversations with me. He'll say, "Well, we can try this new thing if you want, but here are the things that could pop up and kick you in the ass if we do."

Just be sure to come to the table with some knowledge of the compensation structure you want and what you hope to accomplish so you're not completely wasting their time. This isn't your teacher or business coach— expect advisement, not education. Learn the basics here, go to networking events, and find a mentor for syndication basics. Lean on your syndication attorney for deal specifics.

COMMERCIAL INSURANCE AGENT

→ Role: Insures the property, necessary for closing
→ When to find: When you start looking for properties
→ When to engage: Before you make an offer; helps with assessing the deal
→ Type of interaction: Transactional
→ Type of expense: Free quote, first payment at closing

You can run a Google search to find this teammate, too— *commercial insurance agent in Austin*, for example. The best place to find a good commercial insurance agent is to find out who people are using. There are national real estate events happening all the time, and they likely have local meetups on a regular basis as well. Go to all of them that you can. Those events are the main places you'll build your network and get referrals for your team members.

By this point, you can see why it's important to create

some free time to be able to work on your first syndication deal. This works best if you're already retired, or you've saved up enough money to live off of for a year or two while you get this off the ground.

Insurance quotes can take multiple weeks to come through, so you need to engage them shortly after the contract is signed or even to get a high-level quote when assessing a deal. Be sure to interview a few different people and get two or three quotes.

Your relationship with your insurance agent is completely transactional—after closing, you're done interacting with them except in the case of claims and annual renewals. Even when you find someone you like working with, you'll want to compare their quotes against a couple of others on each new deal and even ongoing annually at renewal time, just in case someone can get you a better deal. They'll become your basis for cost, and now and then someone else will be able to do better.

Before you're under contract, shoot a few commercial insurance agents your information and see if you can get a quote. It can be really simple: "We met at this meetup, and you told me to call you if I ever have anything. I'm looking at making an offer on a property—can you give me a high-level quote on what we might get insurance for on it?"

It's important to only work with commercial agents, or they won't know the commercial insurance requirements that your lender has. These loans come with specific requirements for insurance or they won't close on them. Even if you're getting a smaller loan from a local bank, they'll have some requirements. Banks don't want to lend money for properties that aren't properly insured, and everyone has their own idea of what "properly insured" means. So make sure your quotes come from people who will know what needs to be done.

If you pick the wrong guy and don't have proper insurance in place at the last second, you'll wind up delaying close, and your reputation will become one of a person who doesn't have their shit together.

MANAGEMENT COMPANIES

→ Role: Provides ongoing management of the tenants and property needs

→ When to find: When you start looking for properties

→ When to engage: Due diligence period, within a week of the contract

→ Type of interaction: Ongoing relationship

→ Type of expense: Typically free consultation, ongoing operational expense of between 3-10 percent of revenue depending on size of property after close

I self-manage all of my properties through my own management company, but that is not required or even standard for syndicators. In fact, your lender will almost assuredly require a third-party management company on your first deal, since you have zero experience. I recommend at least starting with a third-party company for your first deal, and the time to get one lined out comes pretty quickly after you have an accepted contract.

Just like our other team members, meetups and referrals will send you in the right direction. Find two or three who have decent reputations, and sit down with them to see who's the best fit for you. This can really come down to personality. You know how you anticipate the property being managed—is that how they're going to run it? Will they be easy to work with? Can you envision a good working relationship with these people? What's their fee structure like?

Interview each management company until you find one that you anticipate having a good working relationship with—and get that going as soon as you can. You can have an idea of who you want to interview as soon as you start doing the property search, then narrow it down when you have a property in mind.

Their real work comes after close, but there are items you will want their help or input on earlier on. Prior to close (and even during your underwriting period), they can help confirm your budget and their ability to hit your projections. You can get a budget together that looks great, but if the management company can't run it for those amounts, you're going to be disappointed. Figure that out during due diligence so you don't risk losing your earnest money.

They may even be able to handle the on-site inspections and lease file audit for you. At a minimum, they'll need to be engaged a couple of weeks prior to close to get your books set up.

Some companies will provide budget work for you as a service, and others will do it at no cost. Others will go as far as doing a lot of the budgeting and market survey legwork for a fee, regardless of whether you hire them to manage the property. Outside of that kind of service, as a rule, you won't have to pay anything until after closing. Their fees will be a percentage of the top line revenue before any expenses come out and will be paid to them monthly from the revenue the property generates.

An important thing to understand here is that your property has to support itself and all of the expense of running it. The management company doesn't pay the employees or pay for marketing themselves. You do. The employees will work for the management company and will simply be assigned to your property, but they truly belong to the management company.

BOOKKEEPER AND CPA

→ Role: Keeps your financials accurate and up to date, files taxes, and files tax returns
→ When to find: Midway through due diligence period
→ When to engage: Week or two prior to closing
→ Type of interaction: Ongoing relationship
→ Type of expense: Hourly expense to the business, ongoing

These are probably the most important teammates for the long-term health of your business. At the very least, get a strong bookkeeper who can work with a CPA on the backend when it's tax time. Anything less than that and you're asking for trouble.

You really want someone here who is recommended by other real estate professionals. And we're talking high-conviction referrals here, from people who have worked with them and enjoyed the experience. They should be familiar with what you're doing as a syndicator and able to keep everything in order. It doesn't matter how good you are at organizing the deal and operating the day to day—if your books are a mess, you could be completely screwed. Referrals are key.

It's nice when the bookkeeper says they have experience doing the books of other real estate investors, sends you to them, and the investors agree that they did a great job. That's technically probably enough of a referral. However, I personally like to step that up a notch and get a CPA who actually owns real estate themselves when I can. That's when you know they understand it.

Your bookkeeper/CPA will usually start performing work a couple of weeks before closing. They'll put all of the confirmed investors into the accounting software they use. The day of closing, you'll get a Buyer's Statement that outlines all of the fees and details of the purchase, and they will put that information into the software as well. And of course, they'll continue to keep track of profits, distributions, and tax-relevant details throughout the year as long as you have the property.

I can't stress strongly enough, do not attempt to make these opening bookkeeping entries yourself just save a few dollars. If you screw this up at the beginning, it's going to impact the rest of the project all the way through or cost you a lot of time and money later to fix your mess.

Rent and day-to-day expense/income tracking for the property itself will be managed by the property management company, whether that's yours or the third party you hire. It's separate from the asset management book-keeping that we're talking about here.

If you wait until it's time to engage the bookkeeper to find one, it's too late. In fact, that's true of each of these roles. As soon as you start touring properties, get this loose framework of team members together. Have them on deck so that when they're needed, you won't be stuck scrambling to pull everything together at once.

POST-CLOSING TEAMMATES: TAX PROTESTS AND COST SEGREGATION

→ When to find: After closing
→ When to engage: Tax protests vary by region; cost seg-regation can be up to a year after close
→ Type of expense: Fee-based

We've talked about the teammates that you have to have in place in order to make the deal happen, but there are two more that we can't forget—even though they show up later in the game. This is your clean-up crew.

Within about sixty days after close, find a cost segrega-tion specialist and get something set up for them to do the study for you. It can happen within six months with a backdate to the close date, but if you knock it out right away, you won't have to worry about it anymore.

Again, your best choices are going to come from referrals. Cost segregation people can charge you up to $20,000 for the study, while my guy consistently charges $3,000 every single time. Talk to people who use these professionals and find the ones who do the work well without costing you an arm and a leg.

In Central Texas, property tax assessments happen in the first third of the year, while other states like Tennessee only reassess every four years, and that's when we engage a protest company to get that amount changed—or at least try. If you buy a property that just went through a reassessment, you won't have to worry about it for a while. So look for your local process and make sure that you dispute it when it happens to get that tax expense down as low as you can possibly get it.

You might have experience protesting your personal property tax, but that doesn't mean you should do it for a multimillion-dollar asset with lots of moving parts. Usually, they'll charge you based on how much they saved you in taxes. If they saved you $20,000, they'll charge you a percentage of that total (usually 20–30 percent). If you pay $5,000 and save $15,000, the expense is more than worth it. Don't DIY.

Listen, I promise you that this is all going to be much easier once you've done it a couple of times. Your team will grow. You'll know where to go to find quotes, you'll have the biggest relationships established, and you won't ever have to lay all this groundwork again. It sounds like a lot of work to get there, and it is, but it gets better. Over time, it'll become automatic.

After seeing the amount of work that is going into this and the people involved, I again really want to encourage you to find someone local to help mentor you through this process.

CHAPTER FIVE

NEVER STOP NETWORKING

Way back when I was trying to raise money for my first deal, a guy I barely knew told me he wanted to be my first investor...and he gave me a quarter. It was a tongue-in-cheek way of giving me a placeholder even though he didn't have a $100,000 check to hand over right then. We joke about it to this day, because we're still good friends and colleagues.

Put that way, it all sounds so light and easy, like I just stepped into fundraising and people threw money at me, and now I network all the time without any problems. That's not the case at all.

We've always known there are extroverts—who you'd think could network easily—then the introverts who might have trouble. But then people started in with extroverted-introverts and introverted-extroverts, and honestly, none of it matters. It doesn't matter what title you put on somebody; this shit can be hard.

When I started out in syndication, I knew I had to connect with people to build my team and start raising funds. If you put me on stage in front of 5,000 people, I'm great. I'm not nervous, I'm not worried, I'm totally at home. But the second I walked into a networking meeting where I didn't know anyone in those early days, I would freeze. I can't "work" a room.

Those rooms full of people that I don't know, especially back when I didn't know anything about what I was doing, made me tense up. They still do. It seems like everybody is able to stick around getting to know each other, networking, and connecting, while I feel anxious and uncomfortable. So much so that I just...leave. I literally just turn around and walk out. I would make myself go to whatever the class was, then I would bolt for the door as soon as it was over.

Thankfully, the other side of my personality is a bit obsessive. I learn every possible thing I can about whatever I'm interested in, and I was absolutely interested in syndication. That was enough to keep putting myself in those painful situations until I could handle it enough to make something happen.

I had to learn not to emotionally beat myself up on the way to the elevator after each of those meetings, because that doesn't help at all. Instead, I had to make myself keep going back until the conversations couldn't be avoided anymore. Eventually, enough people caught me and talked to me for long enough that I felt like I knew them, and I could go right to them at the next meeting and sit without feeling like I was all alone. Eventually, I was "assimilated" into the group. The more I learned, the more I felt comfortable in my knowledge base, and that became a comfort too. Eventually, I even started my own meetup, and that's where most of my first investors came from.

I can't tell you there's a completely happy ending there. My personality hasn't changed. I'm not suddenly a fan of small talk or networking in new spaces. In fact, those spaces can still create the closest thing I've ever felt to a panic attack.

Just recently, my wife and I went to an event, and she could tell I was ready to get out of there as quickly as possible. As soon as it was over, we made our way to the door, but a guy stopped me on the way out to comment on my Apt-Guy hat. He said, "I love the hat! That's so creative and clever!"

Later, I was able to verbalize to my wife what had happened in my head. I knew without a doubt that he was opening the door for more conversation about what I do. It was the awkward opening at a singles bar. My job was supposed to be to keep the conversation going and maybe make a connection that works for both of us. I just had to say, "I'm the Apartment Guy, not Apt Guy. I'm not *apt* to do anything..." then lead into a conversation.

I was fully aware of this at the moment, but instead of leading into a conversation, I froze. I laughed awkwardly, thanked him, and got out the door.

I couldn't help it. That's all my brain would let me do.

I'm telling you this because syndication doesn't happen without networking. I know there are some of you who have a gift. You're like a politician who can shake hands and kiss babies and compliment hats all day long. The rest of us can't. I still struggle, even though I manage to get through it because it's what has to happen.

You've come this far in the book because taking on the risk, managing the team, and managing the assets seems doable to you. It's easy to get blinded by the dollars at this point and think you can just grit your teeth and get through the fundraising piece.

The only reason that worked for me is because I knew

who I was. I still know who I am and what I have to work through every time an event comes up. It's not easy and probably never will be, but the payoff is worth it *to me*. If networking doesn't come naturally to you and you can't push yourself through horrifyingly uncomfortable situations like I have, or if the payoff isn't worth that pain for you, it's not going to work.

You have to understand and appreciate who you are. On this one piece alone, syndicating might not be for you. Just like shrinking from risk or responsibility would mean this isn't for you, burning out from social anxiety might rule it out, too. Only you can know.

Keep that in mind as we work through this chapter on what it takes to build your network of investors and call them up when you have a deal.

LEGAL STARTING POINTS

Before we get started here, remember that I'm not an attorney. Consult with one first, before you start networking and raising funds and accidentally do things the wrong way. For the most part, this chapter will assume you are filing a 506(b) with the SEC for your offering, as that's how most of you will file your first deal.

The reason I'm calling this networking and not fundraising is simple: you typically can't actually raise funds before you have a deal, it has to do with the way you structure your deal with regard to the SEC. You can't meet someone today and send them a deal tomorrow. Legally, again, for most filing options, that's not how it works.

You can only present a deal to someone who you have a pre-existing relationship with, who understands what it is to invest in these things, and who you know will be a good personality fit.

Being selective does yourself and the investor a favor, but it goes deeper than that too. In the eyes of the Securities and Exchange Commission (SEC), anything less than that is "solicitation," and comes with hefty consequences. They don't want to see you bringing in just anyone and taking their money to fund your purchases.

When you start working with a syndication attorney, you're going to file with the SEC first, and there are some choices in what you can file. You don't have to register for a full security, because that is prohibitively expensive. Instead, you will likely structure under one of two exemptions—506c or 506b. This is way out into the weeds, but I'm telling you this because 506b will only let you syndicate with sophisticated and accredited investors that you have an established relationship with. You can't do that kind of deal by standing up in front of a room and asking for money. If you haven't connected and developed a relationship with sophisticated investors who have an established understanding of the risks they're taking on, you're not allowed to bring them into those deals.

If you structure yourself as a 506c, then you can run it just about any way that you want to. You can run Facebook ads and stand up in meetups and do just about anything as long as it's not fraudulent, illegal, or dishonest. The catch is that your investors will need to be accredited, which means a million dollars' net worth without counting your personal residence.

These definitions can change, and there are obviously more details you'll want to know. But for the purposes of this book and relaying my experience, these are the two main filings that people use. I'll mostly refer to the limitations around 506b filings since that's more accessible for most people and is what I have personal experience using.

In the last chapter, I mentioned early on that you will always be networking. Before that, I talked about having two to three times what you need in "soft commits." This is why. If a property comes through that you want to take advantage of, you don't get to go meet new people right then. There won't be enough time to build a relationship and get people comfortable with your deal. You have to turn to the relationships you have already built, find out who might be interested, and not all of those people will come through. More on how that works in a minute.

So here's what it looks like to build a relationship first: When you meet somebody, usually at a networking event, you can tell them what you do (you're a syndicator) and exchange information. That's it. To avoid the appearance of "solicitation," you don't get to present anything about deals you're looking at on the first meeting, period. Even if they tell you, "I'm an investor looking for a syndication to be part of a particular kind of deal," you just exchange information. It's not wise to talk about your deal, answer direct questions, or initiate anything investment-specific on the first meeting.

Make the contact, offer your email address, and get them to reach out to you first: "Here's my business card. Send me an email and tell me what you have in mind, you're doing this to establish a paper trail if it ever comes up with the SEC."

That's it. You don't ask them for money. You don't tell them about the deal you're looking at. You don't offer to send them anything—you don't make the first contact by phone or email. They have to initiate the first contact in a documentable, organic way: an email, a phone call, a request to meet up. The SEC is only okay with syndicators who facilitate a deal for investors who are looking, not the other way around. They have to solicit you. If you're ever questioned about why someone was on your deal, you want to be able to point back to the moment that they reached out to you as an investor looking for a syndicator.

Without crossing your Ts and dotting your Is, you might jeopardize your investment and your future in this industry. Don't be tempted to cut corners, even if you're stressed about being able to raise the money. Better yet, don't back yourself into a corner in the first place by making offers without enough potential investors on board.

People are going to bail. Soft commits will fall through. Plan for it. That's why we start with the parameters we do, why we network on an ongoing basis, and why I tell people to get two or three times more than they think they need.

FIRST (DOCUMENTABLE) CONTACT

Sometimes people think raising money means walking into a networking event with business cards and walking out with $2 million in physical checks. That's not it at all. Raising money has to start with a list of potential investors that you have a preexisting relationship with.

After that initial meeting where you gave them your contact information, they're going to send you an email. If they don't, that's the end of it. It's on them to make the first contact, and if they don't, you act like they don't exist. There can't be any follow-up on your part. They make the first contact.

After that, get on the phone with them. If they're local, meet up with them. Just like the awkward conversation opener at a bar, this is still like a dating relationship. You want to figure out who they are, what they do, and what they're like. You're not sitting them down to grill them about their investment ideals any more than you'd ask a first date how many kids they want. Where are they from? What do they do for a living? What experience do they have in real estate?

Nothing about this first conversation has to do with a deal you might bring them. It's figuring out what they know about investing in real estate, why they are interested, if they understand that there are risks involved, and whether this is going to be a good fit. For me, someone who doesn't know any of the industry jargon at all isn't going to be a good fit. When I'm moving a deal along, I don't have the time to teach someone the business of investing. I have to ensure that you're a good student and a sophisticated investor, so I don't want to start from scratch in that relationship.

Syndication is not like investing in the stock market. You

don't give someone your money and hope it goes well. You're forming a legal partnership with the deal sponsor as the operating partner and asset manager. If you're that syndicator, that means you have sole responsibility for the oversight of the deal, but the investors are partners as well. You're not a faceless ticker symbol on a stock exchange for them. It's about relationships, built on trust and liking the other person and feeling comfortable being tied to each other for the next five or ten years. Don't ignore personality clashes, someone with a bad reputation as an investor, or other red flags that might keep you from bringing them into your deal.

GETTING THE SOFT COMMIT

They've reached out to you, you've had some conversations, maybe you went out for coffee. You both feel comfortable working together, and they have demonstrated an understanding of what it means to invest in a syndication.

Even then, you're still not going to get huge checks from people the first time you have a deal for them. When you're getting to know a potential investor, you might ask, "How much would you think about investing if the deal made sense to you?" It's not an easy question for people to ask. This is another moment of self-awareness—can you get specific with people and ask specific questions?

If you run off of assumptions until it's time to present a deal to them and your assumptions ran high, you're screwed. It's your earnest money on the table waiting for investors to come through. Don't think you know what they're going to come up with if you haven't talked about it explicitly. Be direct, and understand that these are only soft commits—not a guaranteed investment.

You have to keep their answers in perspective. Someone who seemed like a big fish and talked about big numbers might only come up with your investment minimum on that first deal and that's it—likely without an explanation. That's all right. The first time out, they're probably going to test you. If it goes well, next time out, they could show up with those hundreds of thousands that you had been hoping for.

By the way, awkward is normal at first, but watch for red flags. If that conversation is so awkward and forced that you can't get any answers, that's probably not an investment relationship you want to be part of. If you can't talk about numbers with someone who will potentially give you multiple hundreds of thousands of dollars, it should be a nonstarter. You can't move forward with someone who won't give you an idea of where they stand. Sophisticated investors are used to being asked this question and will have an answer ready for you. While plenty of first-time investors match up well with first-time syndicators, they may be a little skittish still if they haven't done this before—people taught us not to talk about money, after all. Just remember you're not obligated to hold anyone's hand. If they want to do the uncomfortable thing to make an investment work, they will. If not, move along.

Fundraising starts with getting a rough estimate. If you had a deal that checked all of their boxes, how much would they want to invest? Keep note of it, as well as what it is they are looking for. Many will have criteria for their investments outside of just the returns. Not every property will fit the people who want to invest with you.

MARKETING NEVER STOPS

Unless you get to a point where you're completely done doing deals—as in, you're ready to hang on until those properties sell, put the money in the bank, and live off of it the rest of your life—you can't stop marketing yourself and networking. Even if you think it's going to be another year or two before you do the next one, that means you have a year or two to build up a bigger list of potential investors. The bigger the list, the more you can buy. The larger the property, the easier it is to manage. Scale is the name of the game, and you can't do that without a group of investors who like and trust you.

What does it look like to always be networking? The most

fundamental piece of it is simply in the way you carry yourself. Some personality types interpret that to mean not showing off. They want to be the millionaire next door who shows up in flip-flops and a T-shirt every time there's a meeting. I'll say this: you *can* show up however you want to. You *can* decide not to give a shit what anybody thinks and let the cards fall where they may. It's stupid, though. You're going to limit your pool of investors significantly if you do that.

Think about it like you would for any other professional. If an attorney on your case came to your house to do a personal visit, how would you expect him to show up? How comfortable would you feel if he drove up in a 1973 Volkswagen Beetle with a door missing, wearing shorts, ranting about some political issue, and all-around behaving like a tool? Your subconscious would be screaming *Danger! Something is real damn wrong here!*

There's a uniform to most professions, even if it's not explicit. We know what to expect from someone who is successful at what they do. It doesn't mean you have to wear a suit, but at least get yourself a nice pair of pants, a decent shirt, good shoes, and a nice watch. You're trying to convey confidence, which is hard to do if you look like you just crawled out from under a bridge to get there.

"Dress for success" is cheesy as hell, but I have to reluctantly admit that it's true. Dress to instill confidence in people—especially since this might be their first deal too. They've probably invested in some other things, and someone told them about real estate. Maybe they were even told about syndication specifically. Their interest is piqued, and they are there to learn more. When you make your first impression, when you meet with them after they reached out to you, and when you conduct yourself in public everywhere in between, carry yourself like the professional people trust and want to work with.

It's not just about clothing, either. Our underlying theme of *don't be a dick* shows up again here. Confidence doesn't mean smugness or walking into the room like you own it because you're "the" syndicator. The decision to do a deal doesn't mean you have a leg up on anyone else, and acting like you do won't help your cause. Even if it's their first time on the investment side of the syndication deal, they might be more sophisticated in investing than you are. Some of them will have been the deal sponsor before and just don't want to do it anymore. Have presence in the room, shake hands firmly, mix and mingle—without being the arrogant center of attention.

This extends to your persona outside of networking spaces, too. If you're polarizing, people aren't going to want to have anything to do with you. Don't be overly political, religious, opinionated—don't be a fist-pounding zealot about anything. You won't piss off everyone with your views, but your presentation will turn people off. To me, that signals someone who is irrational, hot-headed, and aggressive by nature. We might connect on your views, but what happens when we see money differently? What's to stop you from lighting me up the way you do others you don't see eye-to-eye with?

Think about how you conduct yourself in coffee shops, on social media, when you're out on the town...If you want to be a miserable human being, fine. Just know that most smart business people will not let you in. You'll only find other people like you, and you can go off to be miserable assholes together.

That brings me to one more point here, about being true to yourself or trying to curry favor. You might have noticed that I don't mince words. I'm always going to cuss, I'm always going to be straightforward. That's who I am by nature. But I'm not going to be polarizing. I might say *fuck* a lot, but it's never directed at anyone, it's just part of my vocabulary/parlance. People work with me because I'm honest, professional, and I know my shit. Carry yourself like that, and you'll make the connections you need to.

Bottom line: be genuine to who you are, and it'll more often than not work out. People can feel or see through your bullshit facade, so just be genuine.

BE COMFORTABLE BEING NEW

The risk of being arrogant has a shadow partner: being too unsure of yourself to do anything at all. That's the problem I had, and it made networking massively difficult. Outside of the internal drive to do the damn thing regardless of how nervous you are, the best way to get comfortable networking is to practice. Practice what you need to say, and practice at as many events as you can get to. Come up with your elevator pitch and run through it until it's second nature. Go to the events even when it's not comfortable. You'll get better at it every day, but only if you're practicing every day.

I can always tell when someone is screwed from the start. When you ask them what they do and it's full of *um* and *I think*, they're toast. "Well, I'm *trying* to be a syndicator, and I think if I can maybe get some investors that this might be what I want to do...I think someone said I should look close to my house so that's probably a good place to start...I don't know..."

You're better off keeping your mouth shut or staying home until you're ready.

The reason we set those parameters earlier in the book and figure out what you're looking for early on is so you can avoid looking unprepared or unsure of yourself. Lay it out. Know what you're looking for. Rehearse it in your head. Confidence doesn't mean you've done it before—it means you are being smart about it as you learn, and you are prepared.

If you have invested in properties before, be clear about your role. Don't tell them you've done a deal when all you've done is invest passively in someone else's deal. Be up front about your actual experience, because if you sucker them in and they find out you don't know what the hell you're doing—and they will find out—they're going to feel misled. A rare worst-case scenario could turn that into a lawsuit, while a more likely situation is your name will get around in a bad way. They're going to talk, and you're going to struggle to come back from it.

When someone asks what you do, be clear. "I'm a syndicator." Period.

When someone asks what you own, be honest. "I don't own anything right now. I'm looking for my first property."

When they want to know what you're looking for, be thorough (without presenting a specific deal you have in mind—remember those SEC rules). "I'm looking for a 1980s construction in San Antonio, probably forty-eight to sixty units that doesn't need a lot of rehab. Nothing greedy my first time out—I know how this goes."

If they ask a question that you don't know how to answer, own up to it. "I don't know, but I will find out."

That's confidence, and it doesn't step into arrogance, either. Don't be that guy. Just know what you're trying to do, and set out to do it.

Remember, you want to make money *for* all of these people. Not *from* them. A by-product will be your own handsome reward, of course, but that's just a piece of it. At the end of the day, this is not about you. This is about the investor. It's about giving them a way to make a better return than they can with other investment types. When they do, they'll bring you more money. They'll bring you their friends. You'll get more deals, more investments, and more growth.

A good syndicator can have a large and positive impact on the world. Our smallest deal right now has forty-four investors in it, and our largest has one hundred. Assuming each of those people have a three-person household, that's hundreds of families who are breaking out of that traditional path and securing their future in a better way. Not to mention all the people I hire along the way, or the hundreds of families living in the properties that I improve and maintain while we own them. Every single deal adds to the thousands of people that are affected by the work that I do. That's my focus. That's why I do the uncomfortable thing and put myself out there over and over again.

That's how you can feel confident in what you're doing, even when it feels new and unusual. It's how you can market yourself without hesitation. Because it's *not about you*. It's just not. You can be someone else's way out and up. Don't let your hang-ups get in the way.

CHAPTER SIX

FIND A DEAL THAT WORKS

The initial parameters of a deal—the specific type of property you want, the risk you're willing to accept, and the price you're willing to pay—are only the beginning. At every point along the way, you'll need to analyze the details as closely as you can to make sure it still works. Getting stars in your eyes will get you into a mess. It'll just be another thing that you've tried that "didn't work," and it could cost you a whole lot.

I'll give you an example of a revelation early on that changed everything about a deal I was working on. It was a B property in San Marcos, about a half-hour south of where I live, and at this point I had several deals under my belt. Each one feels more comfortable than the one before, but still, on every deal, something new comes up that you learn from.

This one fit all of my parameters at first, so I was ready to do the tour. Usually when that happens, I start looking closer at the details before making an offer and getting locked in under contract. The offering memorandum looked good, I had all of my numbers together, and I was running them through a spreadsheet that I use to assess deals. It carries the numbers out five years, modeling out what my assumptions are for the duration of ownership and the sale. It's more or less about underwriting and checking to see if, based on my experienced projections, the deal is going to work.

When I got to the investor return, however, it only came out to roughly 5.5 percent.

I went back to the offering memorandum—which is the brochure that brokers hand out that shows everything about the property, including their financial underwriting and how they think the property will perform. I looked closer at all of their assumed expenses, and everything looked good. Payroll, utilities, marketing, and admin all made sense. I kept looking...and holy shit. The discrepancy was in taxes.

The broker and I were off in our assumption on property taxes, and not by a little bit. We're talking $150,000 short. They were likely assuming the generic 3 percent increase in rent to cover the generalized 2.5 percent increase in expenses annually—but that doesn't include taxes. I've had properties reassessed at as much as 49 percent more than the year previous. Minimal assumptions aren't going to cut it when it comes to taxes.

I still went to the tour, but I brought the numbers up to the broker. He said, "You know what you're doing, so just disregard my numbers."

That was the end of that deal. I couldn't give the buyer what they expected because their assumptions were too far off to make something work. I thanked the broker for showing me the property, and left.

This is a serious stage. Since we aren't dealing with single-family homes, commercial real estate is a nondisclosure industry. You are deemed to be a sophisticated investor and are not afforded the same protections and disclosures as a homeowner. While the broker can't lie, they don't have to tell you anything about the property, it's up to you to discover it. Every assumption has to be questioned and assessed for yourself. If you trust their numbers and they're off significantly on taxes, it'll kill the deal.

I've seen it happen. A friend of mine saw an 80 percent property value increase in his first year of ownership on a two-hundred-unit property. If you don't know how to make a good projection and assessment, you could end up in foreclosure or at the very least having to do a cash call which will seriously impact your ability to raise money in the future.

Be picky. Take it seriously. Walk through each qualification hurdle, one at a time, and if red flags come up at any point, dig deeper, because you may need to walk away.

HURDLE #1: THE 1 PERCENT RULE

Since you're already building out your team, you'll have brokers sending you listings that fit your basic parameters. When one comes through that looks interesting, you don't want to jump right into a showing. There are a couple of things you can do first to make sure it's worth looking at.

The first hurdle is one you can sketch out on a napkin. It's easy but vital: does the rent make sense for the expected sales price?

When you're interested in a property, you can sign a digital confidentiality agreement and get more information from the broker. They'll send over the financials, and from this you can see what they are currently collecting in rent. As a first step, I'm just going to look at actual rent collection.

I roughly follow a 1 percent rule here. If the current rent

is at least close to 1 percent of the per-door asking price, you have something worth assessing in the first place. If the rent is less than 1 percent, there may not be enough room for it to work. So if the seller is asking $90,000 per unit and they rent the units out at $1,000 monthly (which is 1.11 percent), then it may make sense—there's plenty of room before the rent surpasses 1 percent of the unit cost. Keep in mind this is only a rule of thumb and will not always work, it's just the first hurdle I use to know if I should continue looking at the deal.

All we need to know first is whether or not a property is worth looking into. There are so many variables that will come later that your 1 percent may or may not hold up. That's why we have more assessment steps to go through before you put in an offer. If it passes the 1 percent test, I keep moving forward. Next, I start to work through the seller's income statement or P&L (profit and loss) to build out line-item expenses and verify whether the property really can fall within that 50 percent expense norm. This is where having an experienced local mentor will help as they will know roughly what the individual expense items will be for this area. This is also a great time to get back in touch with your mortgage broker to let them know your aspirations of buying an apartment complex are starting to solidify. Look at the deal with them and try to get a high-level, nonbinding quote on the loan you might be able to get.

HURDLE #2: CHECKING THE PROPERTY OUT

The offering memorandum is full of glossy pictures and flattering descriptions. Don't take it at face value. Before you schedule a tour, drive over to see how much magic the photographer actually worked. See whether the neighborhood is appealing or if it's full of liquor stores, payday lenders, and pawnshops. If you can't physically drive by, at least spend some time on Google's street view to see what the area is like. Never assume that the offering memorandum is a true reflection of the property.

Remember, that unlike single-family homes, these brokers don't have to tell you anything about the property. For the most part, commercial real estate is a nondisclosure business, unlike single-family. Of course, if they do say something, it has to be true, but they don't have to say much of anything at all. You're not some guy off the street looking to buy his first home. This is a business, and you're expected to figure things out for yourself.

Let's assume the back-of-the-napkin assessments checked out and the drive-by assessment looks good. Now you can schedule the actual tour with the broker. You can start to deep dive on your numbers whenever you want, but I like to see the property first. At the beginning you may want to underwrite everyone to get the practice, but with experience, I don't want to waste time underwriting something if it doesn't fit what I'm looking for.

When you get there, you might see the roofs are in worse shape than expected or the parking lot is broken up in the back half of the property. Take notes. Remember that parking lot and the condition of the roofs. Write down that 20 percent of the property has peeling paint. Pay attention to the behaviors around the property and note whether you'll need added security. This is all information you'll need to estimate the rehab costs and some of the expenses you will need to account for when you come back to work through the numbers.

On the tour, look at the physical condition of the asset, structurally and aesthetically. Look for obvious evidence of wood-destroying insect damage. If the exterior is made of wood, is it rotted? How much paint needs to be redone? Then look at the amenities. Is the office or onsite gym physically worn down? Is the pool in need of repair?

Tour any unit that they will show you. An asset with 100 percent of the units occupied is a good sign, but unfortunate for the purposes of the tour. You want to be able to see inside to get a representation of what the units are like. Look for how out of date they are, look for safety issues, and look for anything major like water leaks and structural damage. You'll have plenty of chances to come back if you get an accepted offer, so for now, you just want an idea of whether it is worth moving forward.

After you've done this for a while, you'll have an idea of the general cost for each major repair. Your first time out, a lot of this information will be difficult to know. This is why it's so helpful to have a local mentor who has done this stuff before. Ideally, they can come with you on the tour, or at least help you look at your numbers afterward. You won't know how much it would cost to repair half of a parking lot. You need someone with you who can help you build out an accurate estimate of a rehab budget.

HURDLE #3: THE MARKET SURVEY

Another thing you will want to do is a market survey for the property. While you're in the neighborhood for the tour, visit some comparable properties in the same area, basically looking for similar-age properties usually within 1–3 miles with comparable amenities. You don't have to visit every single property in the area.

Find a couple of direct competitors to the asset you're interested in and go check them out. Get a tour of a unit as though you were interested in renting an apartment, and watch for similar details as you did in your target property tour. You're not asking them about occupancy or things that you wanted to know in your first tour— that would tip your hand and give away the "secret shop" you're going for. You just want to get an idea of what's in the neighborhood.

You are looking at the condition of the competition with regard to the overall look and feel, and pay close attention to the curb appeal. You also want to get their street or market rents and see what level of finish the units have to command their asking rent—do they have granite or quartz countertops? Are the kitchen appliances stainless, white, or black? You want to know what level you may need to improve the target property to achieve the rents of the competition if they are indeed higher. This is all information you will need in order to know if you can expect or achieve any kind of premium rents and will help you plan your unit upgrade rehab budget to attain your new target rents.

If your prospective property had Formica countertops with holes and old commercial-looking industrial lights, but its competitors have quartz counters and pendant lights, you have some work to do if your idea is to get the higher rents that the competitors are attaining. Without comparable quality, you're not going to be able to get the rent that everyone else is getting.

This is the market survey. It's looking around to see what the competition looks like. It's getting a full picture of what you're about to buy. Maybe you're already comparable and some simple updates will let you raise rent. However it shakes out, an actual tour is really the only way to get accurate information. Websites aren't going to cut it.

These are not small considerations, either. If you purchased a property based on its own characteristics and merit, then did the market survey after closing to determine how you can update it, you'd miss your opportunity to raise the funds needed for the upgrades before you close and you won't be able to go back to the investors for more money without it causing some real heartburn for them and making your next deal much more difficult to fund. Start here, as you're building out your potential purchase, so that all of the factors can be included if or when you put in an offer.

Let's say you're at $800 per unit in rent to start. The building across the street is about the same age, and they're getting $950 per unit. Look at the factors that make it more attractive to a renter, and know that you will need to reach that level if you want to get that rent. If they are all about the same, rent and everything, then it's just a question of how the numbers play out and whether it would be worth it to you to make some upgrades.

This is also a question of your end game. Do you want to get a property that's beat to shit, 60 percent occupied, and an overall mess? Some people love to get in there and put in the work to clean it up and create a lot of added value. In this scenario, you probably won't be profitable and able to pay distributions for months if not a year or more. This is a fairly risky process, especially for your first inexperienced deal and if the market turns on you before you can execute your plan, you could be in a world of hurt. This is why I don't recommend it for your first deal. Usually, it's best to buy something fully stabilized and operate it very well for your first deal while you really learn this business. It should be making money from day one with a fairly high occupancy rate, and it should be pretty much free of crime and chaos. Learn on something simple that doesn't need too much overhaul or intensive management. This will help ensure you get off on the right foot, and besides, your lender is not going to feel safe in lending to you on something that will be a ton of work and a bit of risk without a proven track record.

THE LETTER OF INTENT

If you've made it through the initial numbers, a decent tour, and a market survey that checks out without breaking your estimated expenses, it could be time for a letter of intent. One thing to keep in mind before going any further is that you should always think about backing out every time a new hurdle is in front of you. Don't get "pot committed," where you don't feel like you can back out now that you've gone so far. Not trying to be overly conservative here, you just need to ask yourself at every step, is this still *really* a good deal or are you emotionally blinded to what the numbers and data are screaming.

If the numbers don't work anymore, they aren't going to get better. If you thought it was an 8 percent return but then suddenly it's 2 percent and you have all this time and maybe even earnest money and up-front costs into it—back out. Eat the loss and move on. If you get into a property with a small margin of error, and things don't go exactly as planned, you could start losing money fast. Once closing is complete, it's not just your money lost, but other people's as well. You don't want that. You are a fiduciary of your investors' money, don't ever lose sight of that.

If you can't stomach losing tens of thousands when walking away is clearly the best decision, you might not be cut out for this.

With that said, assuming everything looks good on the front end, you might be ready for a letter of intent (LOI).

The LOI lays out the high-level terms that you intend to purchase the property under. It varies from person to person, but I like to include a few standard things. You will state your purchase price, the earnest money you intend to put up (rule of thumb is 1 percent of the purchase price but it's totally negotiable), the length of the due diligence period I want, and that I have a right to terminate within that timeframe to get my earnest money back. Usually a small portion of that amount is left for the seller as "option money," around $1,000, just for tying the property up for a few weeks.[2] I also put my anticipated closing date.

At this point, I have done enough of these that I have a boilerplate document with language I can switch out for each deal. For your first few deals, you'll want your real estate attorney to help. It's worth paying them to get the language right.

You're not here to nickel and dime the seller. You're not here to show off and win. So don't try to lowball and play the money game here. Make legitimate offers on legitimate properties, and eventually, you're going to make one work.

Sometimes it takes ten or twenty LOIs before you get one under contract. Some people submit a hundred before anything works out. On the other hand, I got the very first deal I submitted an offer on. Sometimes it happens that way, so take each LOI just as seriously as though it were going to work. It'll get easier as you go, but until then, think of this as practice assessing deals. Commit to it, learn as you go, and see it through.

---

2   As a reminder, expenses like this could potentially come out of your pocket. When you scale up to a $20 million asset, that's a fraction of a percent. If $1,000 is too much for you to possibly lose, you're probably not ready to be a syndicator.

Now shit's getting real. You've had your fun test driving this shiny little car, envisioning what it would be like to have this huge property as part of your portfolio. Now you're making an offer on that shiny toy, and the real work is about to begin.

CHAPTER SEVEN

PUT YOUR TEAM INTO ACTION

Entrepreneurial-minded people are excellent deal sponsors. They can take the risk and they get shit done, and syndicating is ultimately about business ownership. The difference is that we're not sole proprietors. We're not running a startup where a founder can't take a paycheck for a year or two and has to wear every single hat to make ends meet.

You might have been a DIY kind of person in your single-family properties or at the executive level in your profession or as the founder of your own business. That's fine. Lean startups need that kind of self-driven leader. If you're the kind of person who has to turn every wrench yourself and manage every process on your own, you might make it through a six- or twelve-unit property. You would have to learn as you go, research, and do a lot of leg work to cover yourself, but you could manage some side income and a modest life.

When I was working on my very first property, a friend of mine was several deals in. I'll never forget him telling me, "Bruce, if you would just work at this for forty hours a week, you could get another *half percent* return out of it."

Really? A half percent?

That's not the kind of business we're talking about in this book. To reach the potential in syndication—not to mention to protect yourself and your investors—lean on your team. Some people feel like they have to work at something all day every day or they're not doing enough. They don't know how to relinquish control and let their team really shine. When syndication is done well, you don't go into anything on your own. Everything you do is with your team by empowering and trusting them but also following up and holding them accountable, and that team is factored into all of the numbers to make sure that it's going to work.

I told him, "I didn't do this to buy a job. I did it to buy a functioning company."

Syndicating is not the same as a traditional startup, property ownership, or stock investments. It's pulling a team of investors and professionals together to buy a business that has been around for decades, with a proven track record and demonstrated profitability from day one. All we have to do is buy it, get the new staff in place, and just keep running it.[3]

By the time you have a letter of intent in hand, you should have a team of people on the bench, ready to come up to bat. Trust them. Learn how to delegate tasks to the appropriate professionals as they are needed, because that's really the job. Syndicating is about bringing the right people to the table to get the right deal in place. I like to boil it down to one simple, cheesy reminder: you can't grow if you can't let go.

By the way, my friend came around years later. He is learning that hanging onto too much control stunts growth, and that his team is the key to scale. The more deals you do, the easier it is to bring the team together, the easier it is to do more deals, and the cycle goes on. There is definitely a happy medium between wanting to do too much and being an absentee owner who will bury your head in the sand and put it all on your team.

---

3   This is the case for a fully stabilized and well-run property, which is what I believe the first-time syndicator/buyer should do. If, however, this is a rough property that needs to be totally cleaned up and rehabbed, then it will definitely take more than just staffing it and running it.

MORTGAGE BROKER: GET A LOAN

Once you have an accepted LOI, things will start moving quickly. Even as we break down each step and the teammate responsible for it, many of them will occur simultaneously. It's fast and furious for about sixty to seventy days. Let's start with the mortgage broker.

This is your advocate to lenders, hopefully a big network of them. You'll need to connect with the mortgage broker well before the deal begins to get an idea of what size deal you can likely get approved for. On that first call, you'll want to tell them what you're hoping to do and provide them with your personal financial statement, a real estate-geared bio, liquidity verification, and a Schedule of Real Estate Owned (SREO) if you have one. They'll use that information to help you estimate how large a loan you should be able to qualify for yourself. Remember that you're not limited to your own personal wealth and liquidity—you can bring someone else on your loan to help make it work.

Get in touch with the mortgage broker again when you've found a property you're interested in. They can give you some high-level loan numbers that you will use to assess the deal and craft your LOI. Once your LOI is accepted, it's time to go back to them a third time.

This time, they can start to steer the loan process itself. If you ever think it's cheaper to go right to a lender—think again. With a broker, not only do you get the added benefit of their advocacy, you usually aren't paying anything more at all. Typically, the lender and broker split the same 1 percent origination fee no matter who you go through.

Together, you can fine-tune your numbers based on the purchase price and property's financial projections. They'll want to see proof of funds, which will probably include bank statements and brokerage statements. They'll want a more tailored bio too, which should highlight anything that can be related to real estate. For example, if you have managed a P&L for a multimillion-dollar company, include that in your bio as an example of the way you'll manage the apartment project.

For option or due diligence period, while you're crawling all over the property doing your inspections, you'll also be able to make sure your lending will come through. In fact, you can include a "finance contingency" in your offer that runs past the due diligence period, forty-five days is common. If at any point in that period, your lending falls through, you can usually still get out of the contract without losing earnest money, but the devil is in the details. You will want to work closely with your real estate attorney to make sure the wording accomplishes what you want it to.

There's one caveat here: you might not always get that

finance contingency. In a seller's market, they can and often do tell you to figure absolutely everything out within thirty days. That's something to be negotiated. Either way, you want to get lending in motion right away, and get them what they need when they need it. You don't want any surprises outside of those thirty- or forty-five-day windows.

REAL ESTATE ATTORNEY: GET A CONTRACT

While the mortgage broker is busy finding you a loan, the real estate attorney will be going back and forth with you and the seller's attorney to work through the details in the final contract. Your first step with the real estate attorney will be to work on the LOI together. When your LOI is accepted, the real estate attorney will already be engaged and familiar with the circumstances. Next comes the contract for the property. Remember that the LOI is simply high-level or a general outline of what you have in mind for the terms of the finalized and detailed PSA (Purchase and Sale Agreement) or contract.

The real estate attorney is going to help you understand the details of the fifty- to sometimes over one hundred-page contract that will go back and forth between you and the sellers. They will help you understand every single clause, how it will affect you, where something might bite you in the ass, what liability and risk you might have, and more. You can push back on things that the seller includes to find a compromise, and that takes a lot of back and forth.

Until the contract is signed, stay extremely available to your attorney. I've had contracts settled within a week or two, but it can take as much as a month or more. That whole time, your attorney will shoot you questions, need your input, and run things by you. If you take too long getting back with them, the seller could assume you aren't taking it seriously. They can get irritated and pull out of the deal, and without a signed contract, you have no recourse. That's it.

Likewise, you can always go to your attorney for questions. You will, almost without exception, never have direct contact with the seller or their attorneys. This is done to ensure civility and makes for a better and less contentious process. If you have any questions about the property specifically, it runs through the listing broker, and legal or contract questions will go through your real estate attorney.

As a reminder, contract negotiation is typically going to be an hourly expense, and will typically run something like $250-$400 an hour but I've seen over $500/hour for some, and this can amount to $10,000 or more depending on how much back and forth negotiating there is.

After the first deal or two, they might forego payment until closing day. Until then, they will usually want an up-front retainer, ongoing billing, or both.

SYNDICATION ATTORNEY: GET A DEAL STRUCTURED

The first conversation with a syndication attorney will be foundational for your relationship. You'll get a feel for how they operate, what they need from you, and what their timelines are. Bigger firms might only take a few days to get an offering packet together for your investors, but that could look like a couple of weeks in real time. Get a feel for that timing when you get to know them early on, and plan for it when it's time to engage them.

To structure a syndication offering, they don't even need the specific details about the property. They *can* start to put a deal together as soon as you know what kind of property you want to find. However, their services do come at a cost. If you don't close on a property for some time, you'll still owe them the $7,000–$20,000 it costs to craft that deal for you which is typically paid before they start the work. They're sure as hell not going to give you a refund, though if it happens a few times a good person will start to suggest that you think twice first. Those funds are completely out of pocket until the partnership can reimburse you after the deal closes.

The sooner you feel comfortable engaging them, the better—it could take a few weeks to get it together, and you'll need this package in order to raise funds. The safest time is as soon as you have a LOI accepted and you are really confident that the actual contract will be executed. If it takes a couple of weeks for them to get the document back to you for you to redline and finalize, you'll still have space to present it to your investors and get the cash in hand.

Outside of the investors, who are the most important part of your syndication team, this relationship is one of the most important to get right. Even if everything on the real estate contract is buttoned up from a legal perspective, missteps on the fundraising and investor interaction side can create problems.

If the syndication attorney expense breaks your deal, you never had a deal in the first place. Don't let your emotions get in the way. That's easier for me to say now that I've scaled up some, but it's just as true in the beginning as it is ten deals down the road. The syndication attorney is here to protect you in the event that something goes wrong. Doing a deal without a syndication attorney is like playing Russian roulette: don't.

INVESTORS: GET FUNDED

If you're doing this right, you've been in contact with a fair amount of potential investors for a while now. For your first deal, investors will probably put in about $10,000–$50,000 max, and I recommend getting soft commits for two or three times what you actually need, because people are going to back out. That way, long before you have the LOI and contract in hand, you know who you can turn to once it's time to actually collect the funds. They made the first contact, you got to know them and have developed a relationship, and you have them on a list ready to go when it's time.

Remember, in the eyes of the SEC, the relationship comes before the deal.[4] You have to make sure it's a good fit, that they understand the risks involved, and that they know what they are getting into. If that hasn't happened and you are filing as a 506(b) offering, you don't send them the deal.

After you've found the potential investors who are a good fit, you can give them some high-level information on the deal within a week or two of getting a signed contract for a property. It can be as simple as attaching an offering memorandum to an email that says, "We have a deal to look at, and you've expressed interest in the past. If you have any questions, let me know." You can't

---

4   This is for 506b filers, which I talked about in chapter 5.

take any money without the syndication attorney's paper-work, but you can get everyone familiar with the property and opportunity.

It's usually a good idea to offer some kind of presentation and Q&A session as well. I do mine on a live webinar that we record for people who can't make it, and I know people who do theirs locally if all of their investors are nearby.

In the offering memorandum, I include color pictures of the property, information about the location and demographics, the potential we see in it, the projected returns, and a little bit about why we like the deal. During the presentation, I load the memorandum into a PowerPoint and go through it step by step. It takes about forty-five minutes for my wife and me to talk about who we are as sponsors, then go through the presentation, and open it up to questions.

We go as long as it takes to answer everyone's questions, usually for another fifteen to thirty minutes. The goal is to get as many investors interested and comfortable in the deal as you can, as quickly as you can.

As you develop a track record on subsequent deals, people will be quicker to respond. They'll know how you run your deals, they'll like the numbers they see, they won't have any questions and they'll tell you to send over the documents as soon as they're ready. Investors who are new to you, or showing up when you're new, might be a little more cautious. They'll attend the webinar, ask questions, maybe email or call you afterward—it will take a little more to get them comfortable.

Overcommunicating is better than coming up short. Of course, you don't want to bombard them with a bunch of emails every day, but make sure they have the information they need in order to feel comfortable and make a decision. Be up front about everything that they need to know. Probably half of them or more won't invest with you, and that's okay. That's why I tell everyone to raise two to three times what you're ultimately going to need. People who are very interested are still going to bail when it comes time to actually invest. They might love you, but they don't have the money for whatever reason right then. They might not like you, and that's okay too. Give them the opportunity to feel comfortable with you and with the deal, and then let them make the decision.

From the time you get the deal under contract, you have about six weeks to engage the syndication attorney, get the documents to interested investors, and get funds in the bank. I promise this time will go by crazy fast. I like to have everything ready in the bank two weeks before closing, so I know it's all done. When it's time for the funds to come in, I have also learned it's easiest to only accept funds by wire. Checks are a hassle. They have to be taken to the bank, they have to clear, and you're on the hook if they don't.

Make sure the funds go to your company's operating account, not anything personal—even if you're planning to transfer it later. Comingling funds is not allowed, so make sure the funds go directly to the business and the business alone.

INSURANCE AGENT: GET COVERED

Before you submit a LOI and make an offer, you'll want to get your insurance agent to work on the bid for the deal.

The bank will never fund your loan without an insurance policy in place, so as soon as you have a signed contract, you need to get things finished up with the insurance agent. Get both your insurance agent and lender's insurance department the information they need quickly, and they will be in touch with each other. As the buyer, they will reach out to you if they need details from the seller. One of those documents might be a "loss run," which is a history of claims from the last three to five years. Usually that will come back clear, and sometimes you'll learn something new.

Engage this process early on, because it can take a while

for all of the people involved to communicate back and forth. For example, the loss run involves the agent asking you to ask the broker or real estate attorney to ask the seller to ask their insurance agent for the loss run. It's a standard, simple enough process, but I've had it take two to four weeks, sometimes more, to get it done.

Don't assume that a simple relationship like this one can be skipped over. If you don't follow the steps in chapter 4 to get a commercial insurance agent—maybe just assumed that your buddy Fred who does your home and auto insurance could handle it—you'll run into the consequences pretty quickly. They're going to tell you they don't do commercial, and you'll have to start from scratch with a looming close date and a process that can take weeks. If you wind up delaying close, the seller could send you a letter of non-performance, keep your earnest money, and walk away or at best, extend the close date, but that usually comes with more earnest money to be put down or even a price increase on the property.

They're probably not going to do anything outrageous, but it's not uncommon to see the price of a property jump by $25,000 or more, or additional earnest money requested in order to get an extension on the close date. It's a good idea to be diligent from the beginning and avoid that headache for everyone.

For the most part, the agent is going to work with the lender's insurance department directly to work out the type of coverage, deductible, valuation, and any history they have to take into consideration. They'll check with you to make sure you're comfortable with the valuation and premiums, but the biggest interaction happens with the lender. If the lender doesn't think the coverage is adequate, they won't let you close.

CPA AND/OR BOOKKEEPER: GET ORGANIZED

As soon as you have a contract, let your bookkeeper know that it's almost time to get started. By the time investor money comes in—right around two weeks before closing—they will need to enter them into your software for year-end tax returns. They also need to be available to input the details from the closing statement on the day you close. If you get off on the wrong foot with accounting, it's hard to catch up.

From then on, their responsibilities are to cover the asset management accounting at the actual partnership level. They'll create opening statements, keep track of distributions, and prep for the annual tax return. Your responsibility will be to provide them with what they need to track to ensure your books are always in order.

Don't cheap out on this role, either. H&R Block is a horrible idea. You need a true bookkeeper or true accountant who has done real estate with partnerships. Each of those layers is different. Get someone as specialized as you can so that they can keep your organization on track.

PROPERTY MANAGEMENT: GET OPERATIONAL

On my very first purchase, I kept the existing management company on board after we closed. While I did interview them to make sure there wasn't anything overtly weird going on, I didn't interview anyone else. I didn't want to deal with finding another company on top of everything else I was doing to close my first deal and the property was being run well under their management.

When I interview—which doesn't happen anymore now that I run my own management company—I'm looking for holistic, character-based things. Do they share my values? Do they understand that we are not slumlords? Are they going to be responsive to the residents? Of course, they can tell you anything they want in an interview, so it's good to go see the properties they run. If you can, secret shop them.

Look at the way the properties are maintained. Pay attention to the way the staff treats you and anyone else who comes in. Are you greeted when you walk in the door? If you say you're looking for an apartment, do they show you one? Do they show off the amenities? If not, or if they act annoyed by you being there, this might not be the management group for you.

In the interview, get an idea of how they run things from a financial standpoint. What kind of reporting do they send? Are you going to get bank account statements to make sure everything is above board and there aren't needless expenditures? Do they make sure their various properties don't comingle financially? Do you have access to P&L statements? At a minimum, I believe you should see a rent roll, trailing 12-month P&L (T12), general ledger, check register, balance sheet, delinquency, and whatever else you feel is important for you.

I also would like them to look at my underwriting and budget and see if they agree with what I have come up with or even better, if they can underwrite the deal themselves for me. This will let me know if they know what they are doing and if experienced, whether they think my numbers look attainable.

When you find a company that checks out, if they aren't managing the property already, they're going to have to have time to staff the property before closing. They'll also need to set up contracts for service providers, like pool service, trash pickup, landscaping, utilities, and more. Make sure they have plenty of time to get everything in place: conduct interviews in the early stages, at or before the LOI. Have someone hired no more than a week after the contract is signed.

As a bonus, some management companies will do the due diligence inspections for you. It's not for everyone— not all syndicators want that, either. But it's something to keep in mind. Either way, they can help you work the budgets to make sure the numbers you came up with are solid. In the right circumstances, this can be helpful as early as the first assessments.

The management company will have its own bookkeeping for all of the day-to-day operations for the property. They'll keep records and generate reports for leases, evictions, work orders, deposits, etc., and they should be getting reports to you monthly, or they need to connect directly with your bookkeeper with this information.

Remember that you hired them to do a job, so don't undermine them in it. Let them run the property. Communicate with them if you see something being mismanaged, like someone not at the office when you dropped by or an amenity in disrepair. Check in with them and find out what's going on and what needs to happen to fix it—but only within the right hierarchy.

The staff are employees of the management company,

not you. You have no right to fire anyone or to tell them to fire anyone. If things aren't going well, you may get to a point where you need to change management companies entirely. You will likely need to get with your lender to see if there is any approval or notice to be given in this instance. They will usually want to know that you have a professional management company to get that first loan, and if something changes, they'll need to know about it. As your largest partner in the project, the lender has a significant say in the way it is run. Keep them in the loop and maintain a good working relationship with them just like any other partner.

Outside of staying in contact with your property management team, you'll make sure your bookkeeper always has the details they need. You'll engage your cost segregation specialist to make sure you're structuring depreciation in the most advantageous way. Depending on the time of year that you close, you'll engage someone to protest property taxes. Then you'll reach out to your investors annually, quarterly, or monthly, following the updates and distribution schedule that you and your syndication attorney laid out. But practically, that's it. The big lift will be done, and you will have a property under your belt.

DELEGATION AND OWNERSHIP

Running your own property management company will

skew this significantly—that's a separate business that you'll need to learn how to run, and it probably will look more like a startup at first. But assuming you hire a third-party management company, you'll be the asset manager from here on in. That means keeping an eye on the financials, keeping in touch with the investors, and getting out in front of potential issues. You'll need to review the monthly and quarterly financial reports that come in from the management company. The bookkeeper will keep the numbers—it's your job to review them to spot any problems before they reach critical mass.

You'll always need to network and fundraise for every single deal. This is a role that people tend to want to outsource. That's fine, but think about how much of the pie you're going to lose if you do that. For my money, it's better to hang on to that responsibility yourself if you can. All of the underwriting meetings, all of the investor relationships, all of the closing requirements are on your shoulders. You can outsource much of this but again, someone will need to be paid or compensated for that and as a startup, it might not be feasible.

On my first deals, signing the contract meant my work was really about to start. Now that I have some scale, I have staff members do a lot of this for me. They schedule the feasibility inspections, figure out the contracts, manage invoices from each contractor and professional we work with, and perform a good deal of the legwork that happens from contract to close. My role is to be the go-between for my company and the broker.

In other words, if you scale enough, you can bring in team members for whatever you want or need. You can have Johnny finding deals, Fred assessing and underwriting them, Mary working through quarterly distribution and newsletters, a regional manager (if you are self-managing the properties) doing the due diligence and inspections...

The first time or two out can be overwhelming. The more you do, the more you'll learn, until it's like muscle memory. Eight years down the road from that first deal, I have a corporate organization that I'm able to support financially while they do most of the leg work for me. I don't spend nearly as much time on the day-to-day business as I did at the beginning. My job now is more on the networking and deal-finding part of the business. My wife and I give ourselves six-figure pay raises every time we buy a new property, provided that is that we have the investors lined up and we can find a deal that works. This is why you never stop networking and growing your investor database.

Today, my wife and I don't have any concerns about retirement, paychecks, burnout, or someone laying us off. We're pursuing our dreams of creating resources and a better lifestyle for our autistic daughter and her peers. We've built more than we could have dreamed of—there's no way my little attempts at business ownership could have changed my life that much, much less within a decade. Syndication is unlike any other investment platform out there. It's about scale, reliability, and a direct reward for your willingness to take on risk and coordinate moving parts.

Syndicating is a bitch, but damn if it doesn't pay off in the end.

CONCLUSION

The most tangible stress of managing a syndication deal happens prior to close. You're taking care of a lot of moving pieces and are responsible for a lot of money for a lot of people, and that's a lot. Once the deal closes, that's it. There's not a lot happening at that point.

That doesn't mean the stress has ended. The more experience you gain doing deals, the more prepared you're going to be for the weird things that come up—and something will *always* come up. Remember when I lost $5.2 million to OFAC? I was completely blindsided that first time, and as I'm writing this book, it happened again. Yep.

Of course, this wasn't my first rodeo. Just as before, I was in progress on a deal, and at the end stage where I needed to get my money in (or I'd be in default and on the hook for all $150,000 of my earnest money)—yet again, the wire didn't show up. Thanks to that fiasco back at the 250-unit property in San Antonio when the wire company told me "it's in regulatory review," I knew what that phrase meant. This time, I could ease everyone's minds a little bit without making them wait. Even better, the seller was understanding about it all. That was good news because they could have held me to it at the closing table anyway, and I would have been liable.

Taking that responsibility on your shoulders is part of being a syndicator. Even after closing, when the property management company is taking care of the day-to-day and all you're managing is assets, you're at the top of the chain. Everything is *your* fault. You hired everyone either directly or indirectly, and the buck stops with *you*.

Just recently, I was served in a discrimination lawsuit for something that happened on one of the properties. We won the case, but when someone goes after the property for any reason, they're going to keep going until they find the person making the most money and responsible for it all. They will try for the employee, the manager, the management company, and ultimately, the owner or ownership group, and you are the managing member of that entity.

I'd say about 40 percent of the people who I've seen do

their first syndication deal never come back to it again. They want to sell it as soon as possible and then walk away forever. The stress and liability from beginning to end is just too much, and I get it. It's not an easy thing we're doing here.

I stick around because the impact is worth the stress. At the end of the day, my wife and I see ourselves as job creators. Not only are we making money for ourselves and our investors, but we're supporting the management company, everyone on our team, and even the people who live in the apartments. I like to think we're playing some part in improving their lives by giving them a better place to live.

And listen, for the right personality, the challenge can also be fun. I'm a deal junkie and don't see myself walking away any time soon. You might be up for it too. Or you might try it once and decide to use what you made to invest in someone else's deal rather than take on another deal. Or maybe you already know that you'd rather just invest from the get-go. I think that's great.

Syndication is a powerful tool—again, not just for real estate, but for anything—that can bring people together to create an impact that they couldn't have made on their own. However you decide to be part of that is fantastic. As long as you know what you're getting into.

HOW TO BE A GOOD INVESTOR

If you know that you'd rather just invest, use what you know now from this book to help vet syndicators and get involved in the right kind of deal. Everything we've talked about from the syndicator side is true for the investor— you're entering into a business partnership. It's important to find one where you get along and can work together. Really, it's a lot like courtship. If one person is in love and the other person isn't into it, you're not going to get very far.

The best way to get to know someone is to just spend time with them. That's a little more challenging if you live in a different state, which is not uncommon. Some people fly in to have coffee, while others may just do it through multiple phone calls to get to know each other. You'll know pretty quickly if you connect with them and if they seem to know what they're talking about.

You can ask them for references, but it's obviously in their best interest to send you to the investors that love them. It's much better if you can connect with their previous investors organically. Just like a syndicator networking for investors, you'll want to show up at events too. Get in their circles of influence and see who knows them and who has been part of a deal with them. It's hard to judge a syndicator by the return an investor has seen, but there's a ton you can learn by just talking to people. How are they at communication? How honest are they? How consistent and reliable are they? If the investors have had a hard time with that syndicator, think twice before jumping into a deal with them.

Common sense wins the day here. See what public information is available about that person, and let that tell you a little bit about who they are day to day.

And remember, all of this applies to you as an investor as well. A good syndicator is checking you out too. Not only are they looking into all of those same character indicators, but they're watching how you interact with them. If I've got forty people on a webinar and there's only one person asking me dozens of questions they should already know the answer to, guess who *isn't* getting invited to the deal? I'm not going to go with someone who appears to be high-maintenance and skittish. As much as you want to work with a syndicator who knows what they're doing, the syndicator wants to work with an investor who is educated in investing and isn't going to be high-maintenance.

By all means, ask the questions that are important to you. Someone once asked me how I "felt" about a concrete plant being down the street from a property. How I *feel*? The property has been there for thirty-five years and so has the plant. What am I supposed to feel? The question meant absolutely nothing to me, even though it clearly meant something to them. That's going to happen. If you can't find the answers and you need them from your syndicator, do what you need to do in order to feel comfortable with the deal. Just understand that you might not be a good fit for that syndicator. It's a two-way relationship. Don't get too stressed about it, because there will always be another deal, provided you are consistently networking.

Like syndication, the more you invest, the more you'll learn what's really important to you. Finding and getting through the first deal will always be the most challenging and unnerving.

Network constantly. Don't be a dick. Be a good human. Eventually, you'll find the right fit and will be able to enjoy the fruits of your efforts.

THE REAL TRUTH ABOUT SYNDICATION

If you're a little overwhelmed right now, good. I told you there wouldn't be rainbows and lollipops here, and there aren't. There's a way to scale your income and your impact. There are plenty of reasons to find a way to get involved. But it comes at a price that not everyone is willing to pay.

It used to be the norm that syndicators were syndicators

because they loved it and were good at it and had gained a ton of experience over time. Now that word has gotten out and everyone is giving it a shot, there are a ton of people who are syndicators but only have one or two deals under their belts. There aren't many of us, percentage-wise, who have stuck around long enough to get those ten thousand hours in.

Everyone is enticed by the money and opportunity, and I get it. But if you're not clear on the challenges in front of you, you're going to be in for a surprise. Even having an idea of the process doesn't really prepare you for the fast-paced challenge that comes with responding to every weird thing that pops up.

If you're still with me even after the disappearing money and random lawsuits and constant networking and analysis: Welcome. It's time to get to work.

There are real estate events all over the country; sometimes it seems like there's one every week. You no doubt have local meetups happening around you all the time. Start to tap into those networks if you haven't already, and look for other syndicators and investors. Get to know what's happening in your area. Go to as many regional and national real estate conferences and events as you can.

Maybe you've avoided those meetings so far because you

got burned by someone selling you pie-in-the-sky promises before. Don't let that scare you away. You don't have to invest in anything that doesn't make sense to you, but you do have to connect with as many people as possible. Just keep your bullshit radar turned on. Vet everyone who steps on stage, and meet as many people in attendance as you can. Networking is key here, so get out there right away. Most people in this industry are great but like any space, you will encounter many that may not have the best of intentions and are just trying to make a buck off of you.

Best case scenario, you'll meet someone who can mentor you in syndication. Check them out the same way you would if you were investing with them, but this time make sure they also have a ton of experience. There's no way I could have helped mentor someone after one or two deals. Hell, I'm still learning things years later. If you find someone you click with who has a strong track record, stick by them and learn all you can. Your first deal will be much easier with someone you can turn to along the way.

If you want to watch a syndicator in action, snag some resources, or catch me at an event, start with apt-guy.com/resources. There you'll find my social media accounts, extra material that goes with this book, and updates on where I'm at and the things I'm continually working on.

Listen, I love syndication, stress and all. I love what it can do for the world, and I'd love to see more people on board. But only if you're ready.

I'm sick of seeing sugarcoated introductions to syndication that get people in over their heads, lose money, stress everyone out, and make a bad name for what it is we're doing. So if you want in, great. If you know now that it's a terrible fit for you, even better.

Find the spot that works for you, your family, and your future, and go after it. There's a place for you at the table, and when you find the right one, nothing will ever be the same again.

ABOUT THE AUTHOR

Known in the real estate world as the Apt-Guy[SM], **BRUCE PETERSEN** is a serial syndicator who started with a 48-unit building and has now syndicated over 1,100 units. As the founder and CEO of Bluebonnet Asset Manager LLC and Bluebonnet Commercial Management, Bruce has received local and national recognition for his syndication efforts. He was the recipient of the Austin Apartment Association's Independent Rental Owner of the Year for 2016 and the National Apartment Association's Independent Rental Owner of the Year for 2017. In addition to being a TV personality and public speaker, Bruce also mentors people on how to invest in apartment complexes.

CPSIA information can be obtained
at www.ICGtesting.com
Printed in the USA
LVHW012030140520
655573LV00008B/98/J